DEDICATION

To CHIEF THOMAS J. LYONS who was my inspiration. My intense admiration, deep devotion and affection for him knew no bounds. His influence on me from the first day we met was immeasurable. He was my idol!

Library of Congress Cataloging in Publication Data
Schneider, Edwin F.

A Fire Chief Remembers - Tales of the FDNY
Library of Congress Catalog Number: 92-070935
ISBN 0-925165-10-7

Published by Fire Buff House, Division of Conway Enterprises, Inc.
P.O. Box 711, New Albany, Indiana 47151
© Edwin F. Schneider, 1992

Printed in the United States of America

A Fire Chief Remembers

Tales of the FDNY

By Battalion Chief
Edwin F. Schneider, Ret.

Fire Buff House Publishers

New Albany, Indiana

FORWARD

My inspiration to compile these tales comes from a desire to share my own fire buffing days and my initiation into and experience in the fire department in New York City, particularly Brooklyn.

I had many pleasurable hours doing this, recalling those memories of yesteryear - mostly pleasant, some painful - the bittersweet recollections were all part of the whole.

It was a privilege and a pleasure to have served and worked with many fine, decent, kind and compassionate men. Notable among them was my dearest friend of many happy memories, Chief Thomas J. Lyons, for whom I had great respect and admiration. Conversely, sorry to say, there were others who were just the opposite. These tales are of both kinds.

EDWIN F. SCHNEIDER
Battalion Chief, FDNY
(Retired)

Fireman Edwin F. Schneider in 1932 soon after he joined the FDNY. After a career spanning 34 years he retired in 1964 as a Battalion Commander.

CONTENTS

PREFACE

The dictionary defines *fate* as a divine decree, or a fixed sentence, by which the order of things is prescribed.

Destiny is that which is to happen to a particular person or thing; the predetermined course of events; the power which determines the course of events.

I probably have become obsessed with a persistent feeling, idea, or the like, which seemingly I cannot escape, and that is that fate and destiny have preordained and predetermined the course of events in my life and existence. This is how and where it all began for me:

On June 15, 1904, the girl who was to become my mother wanted to go on a church picnic boat ride. Her mother (my grandmother) refused to allow her to go, and my mother shed many tears because she was forbidden to go. She told me this story in a Lutheran Cemetery, in front of the monument erected to the memory of the 1,030 people who perished on that excursion boat by drowning and fire. The ill-fated steamship *General Slocum* burned and sank in the East River as it steamed northward from downtown New York City. It was New York City's worst fatal fire ever. Perhaps my mother-to-be may have been a casualty if she were allowed to go that day. The cold chill of the cemetery added to the effects of my feelings as I stood there by her side hearing that story.

The realization that I owed my life to my mother's mother stunned me beyond belief. Had my mother died that day of the tragedy I would not have been born! Is it not ironic that the fire spared her, and my destiny was the New York City Fire Department? Why was I not burned to death when I operated at a four alarm fire when I was Captain of Engine 226 and just missed a sea of fire trapping me by seconds? That instance is forever in my mind - "Destiny!"

There were some 350 companies in the New York City Fire Department when I was appointed. Here we go again - another instance of destiny - I was sent to Engine 220 in Park Slope, Brooklyn. It was there that I met my wife to be; had I been sent to any of the other 349 units; we would never have met. I often relate that to my wife, Rita, and our children Joan and Edwin, that we all owe it to that appointment and to Engine 220!

CHAPTER ONE

THE FIRST OF 25,000 RUNS

There they sat, back in 1929, the men of Brooklyn's Engine Company 240, matter of factly reading a paper and playing pinochle. They had no idea I was hoping and praying for an alarm to bang in. My excitement was at fever pitch; yet I tried my best not to show it.

As time went by and we didn't move, I had the feeling like it was the end of the world - chance was passing me by - my great privilege was evaporating and being wasted.

The bell system of alarms sent out by the dispatcher and received in all firehouses in their respective boroughs was made up of taps and spaces. The men knew their area boxes, and when a box came in, the area's first two digits alerted all hands, putting everyone "on the ready." There wasn't any selective dispatching for areas only (that came years later). An alarm was received twice on the large bell (primary circuit) and once on the small bell (the secondary circuit). A large bell was at the watch desk, and in the kitchen and bunk room.

The alarms kept coming in for all other parts of the borough - our first two digits ("one" and "five") weren't among them. Then - Bingo! - a "one and five" hit in, and everyone was up and running for the apparatus, on the ready. We ran for our gear while the rest of the box hit in, and the housewatchman gave the call "Turn Out - First Due," announcing the location. The chauffeur started the apparatus as Captain Casey slid down the pole, running for his gear next to his seat on the engine. He looked at the back step, saw all was in readiness, gave the order to open the doors, and gave the command to respond. We were on our way - my first run!

The thoughts were always: "What have we got?" The men were looking upwards in the direction of the response area; they were looking for smoke, which would tell them there was a "worker." It would be impossible for me to relate my feelings of the thrill I was experiencing. I held the handrail over the back step, as I was told to do, tightly gripping the bar. There was a fireman on each side of me, wedging their bodies against mine on the back step of the old American La France Pumper. The rigs didn't have a muffler on the exhaust, and the roars of the engines could be heard blocks away; the siren and bell were sounded by the captain while responding.

Everyone on the apparatus knew that we were first due, and no time was lost in getting there before the other units which were also responding. It was unthinkable to have a later unit get there ahead of you and "take your fire." As we pulled up to the box, the excited civilian who had pulled it didn't have to show us where the fire was - we could see the smoke pouring out of the cellar of an apartment house.

The captain ordered the chauffeur to stop at the hydrant and hook up; while that was taking place he gave the order to stretch a hoseline to the side entrance ramp leading to the cellar. The building - a newer type apartment house, was a four-story multiple dwelling, about 50 x 75 in area. (I now know these types are Class 3 - non-fireproof - brick and wood joists.)

I helped the men pull the hose from the apparatus. When enough hose was off, it was uncoupled and the nozzle put on. The skipper was down in the cellar, and we followed with the line. He had found the location of the fire. We heard him but couldn't see him through the dense smoke. We advanced towards his voice, crawling down in a low position, finally reaching the fire area, which was a large storage section used for discarded mattresses, old furniture, rugs, etc. As we knelt at the entrance to this room, the smoke was pouring out, and we could see the mass of flames. The water was started in the hoseline; one fireman controlled the nozzle, with another man on the other side of him; I was right behind the "nozzle man," with the captain with all of us. We were now lying on the floor as the captain ordered the line opened up, and advanced us into the fire, hitting the fire with our line over our heads, onto the ceiling all over the room, which was heavily involved with fire and extremely smokey.

There weren't any masks in those days as there are today; we got deeper into the fire area. Soon we could hear the side windows of the cellar breaking as the truck units began to ventilate. The ranking officer (our captain) is always in command until the arrival of a superior officer. As the other officers of units arrived, they reported to our captain, who ordered them to search, ventilate, and examine upstairs over the fire. The chief arrived and determined the fire had not extended and was confined to the area involved. (Years later when studying, I soon found out the potential of possible spread of fire through vertical openings in these apartment cellars.)

The chief took command, gave the necessary orders while examining for any spread of fire, and in due time overhauling operations were started. The chief was from another battalion - we were out of our own chief's response area - but of course he knew our captain very well. But he didn't know *me* - I had on helmet - boots - and rubber coat - so I looked like a fireman. I kept his vision away from me - continuously turning myself away from where he could look at my face. He and our skipper talked all through the "mopping up" operations and "washing down." When all was finished, the chief gave our captain a "well done Mike," and we were told to "take up" (go back to quarters). I sure was relieved to see the chief go without seeing my face - because the simple truth was that *I was not a member of the fire department!*

CHAPTER TWO

"YOU WERE GREAT!"

It was a warm summer day, and the doors of the firehouse were open. The year was 1914, and as a five year old boy, I was filled with excitement as my father took me for a walk to the neighborhood firehouse. I held his hand tightly, and with awe and fear I looked inside the doors. There was a fireman sitting at a desk near the front entrance. That was the "housewatch" desk. In the center of the floor was a fire engine, and to the side of the engine were horses. The fireman's mustache was big and black; he came toward us, greeted my father, and giving me a gentle pat on my head said hello to me. Of course I don't remember what they were talking about, but it led to us going inside the firehouse. There I was on this hot summer day, standing in front of the big fire engine, scared to death! I dared not let go of my father's hand; the horses looked larger inside than from where I first saw them from the sidewalk!

There was more talk between the men, and then we walked back to the entrance and the watch desk. The fireman took my free hand - (I was still holding onto my father's) and gave me a soft handshake. We thanked him and left. I was thrilled and fascinated by the experience of that day. I'll never forget that one big white horse! The engine (of course I didn't know what it was) was a steamer, which was the forerunner of motorized apparatus. Ironically - believe it or not - that firehouse was the one I was first assigned to many years later, as a "probie" - Engine Company 220 Park Slope Section of Brooklyn - on 11th Street.

My buffing days didn't consist of horses and steamers, although the "old-timers" told me many stories about them. The last run, and the farewell to horseflesh in the N.Y.C.F.D. was on December 10, 1922, when Engine 205 - Boro Hall Brooklyn - responded to Court and Jorelemon Streets. Engine 205 was selected for the last horse-drawn run because that company had been the first in Brooklyn to have a horse-drawn pumper - the first shall be last! That was in 1856, when a group of men in Columbia Heights organized the company known as Pacific Hose No. 14, located on Love Lane.

There have been many stories written about the era of horses and steamers, which were the pioneer days of firefighting. Those of us who came into the department after those bygone days never knew what it was like to spend long hours at night on housewatch duty, looking after and tending to the horses.

The firemen knew what the horses meant to the officers, (especially the captain) and the horses were given the best of care and grooming. Many hours were spent talking to the horses, giving them a drink, and remaking their straw bedding. If by chance a horse happened to be neglected by some fireman who forgot about it because he was "in the books" studying while on watch duty, a horse would sometimes kick the side of the stall, which would awaken the officer upstairs in his office. Many an officer would hop out of bed and call down the pole hole, "Hey down there - give that horse a drink! What's the matter with you!"

There were reprisals and disciplinary measures taken against firemen for neglecting the horses. The thinking was, it took years to train a horse, but only weeks to train a new man.

Five-year-old Edwin Schneider visited a Brooklyn Engine Company such as this one in 1914 with his father. Fire horses in the FDNY answered their last alarm in 1922.

There was a continuous duty hours system of working in those days, with one day off in ten, plus meal leaves. Our beloved Lieutenant Whalen would enjoy reminiscing about his early days when we were just starting out on the job. Once he had his day off taken away from him by his captain for a minor infraction of neglecting to care for a horse!

In general, the firemen were kind and thoughtful towards the horses. The failure to wrap a blanket around a horse upon arrival at a fire during cold weather was just too bad for the driver. That's where the buffs came on strong, blanketing the horses. Many drivers of horse-drawn engines later became motorized chauffeurs; the nerve and daring, plus their quick judgment of distances held them in good stead behind the wheel of a roaring motorized apparatus.

In 1918 the job went into the two platoon system - 84 hours a week - (from the continuous duty work week of 168 hour work week.) In 1898, Brooklyn was consolidated with the rest of New York City, and the annexation absorbed the old Brooklyn Fire Department into the greater city of New York Fire Department. It was great and intriguing listening to the old-timers' stories of those by-gone days, particularly when I was chief's aide to my dearest friend and boss of many happy memories, Chief Thomas J. Lyons, who came into the department January 1, 1910.

In reading about the early history of fire departments, and the horse and steamer replacing the "hand-drawns," one finds those eras very colorful, exciting, and interesting; it was also an emotional time for the members. Many new volunteer companies were organized; there were fist fights over who would have use of a hydrant. Politics played a big part, as members and ward leaders grew more prominent in various neighborhoods.

Watching the horses pull a steamer, with sparks flying form their hooves as they raced over cobblestones with smoke belching from the boiler was an awesome sight. Today, men spend a lot of money searching old barns looking for an antique steamer; much work is then done restoring it. You can see them in fire department parades, horse-drawn and all, polished to perfection - they are beautiful! At an annual get together of antique apparatus at Valhalia, New York, a steamer drafted water in nine seconds, and discharged a stream of water equal to a motorized pumper.

Over the years in my time on the job as an officer, I've seen small boys with their fathers visiting firehouses, usually on a Sunday morning. I could always visualize myself in their places, recalling the politeness of the fireman to my father and me; it was easy for me to treat visitors the same way. As I said, I did not know who the fireman was who patted my head as a small boy; it would have been real special for me to know him years later, when I was appointed to that very firehouse of my first visit.

In my teens we had moved to a neighborhood called Windsor Terrace, near Prospect Park. I soon found myself standing in front of Engine Company 240 on Prospect Avenue. I learned that the firemen would ask boys to go to a store for them, and soon I was given that privilege. It was an advantage enjoyed by a few of us young boys who were favored to run errands for the firemen.

Soon I knew the names of many of the men, and of the two company officers, Captain Michael Casey and Lieutenant George Oates. There was one other youngster like myself and two adult men, who also "hung around," as it was called. The two men were allowed inside of quarters; we two young ones weren't allowed inside for a long time to come. I was content going to the stores for them, getting to know them, and chatting with the men, mostly the man on housewatch duty.

I'd keep the housewatchman company, and listen and learn to count the alarm bells as they were transmitted from headquarters. When I was about seventeen years of age, Lieutenant Oates would allow me inside of quarters - the kitchen in the back room - that was the sitting room to the firemen.

The back room was still off limits for me with Captain Casey when he was on duty. I would always be outside on the sidewalk then, and my "hanging around" did not go unnoticed by the captain, who seemingly to me was a stern man, but liked. Occasionally, he would speak to me, and of course that made me feel good. However, I always knew my place was outside, and never was hinting, looking, or asking to be allowed inside, nor did I let him know the lieutenant allowed me inside. Inside the firehouse for me with the captain was "off limits" for a long time to come.

At home, I'd tell my parents how nice the firemen were to me, and at holiday times my mother would make sandwiches for the men. By now my friend Mel Dunn, the other buff, and myself, were the "official gophers." During the summer months, I was an errand boy for the neighborhood butcher; I'd get the order from the men - they were good cooks - then deliver it to them. This was

when they were working the long day - "Twenty Four."
I marvelled at their cooking a big meal, and was so
pleased with myself - I was their buff!

My life as a buff was completed when one day
Captain Casey, talking to me very casually, sent me into
shock! He told me he knew I was really interested in
becoming a fireman, and he had heard I was going to
Delahanty School taking the fireman course for the next
examination. He told me he was "a little short" of men on
his tour. He said for me to get a helmet, boots, and rubber
coat from the clothes rack of the off duty men, place them
on the engine, and I was to ride with them! My reaction
was one of disbelief - this was unheard of! Even the two
men buffs and Mel, the other buff like myself, never had
that opportunity. I tried recovering by saying "Thanks"
to the captain, and got the gear and placed it in position
on top of the hose, with the boots on the floor at the
ready.

The skipper than went into the sitting room and
told the men he was allowing me "to ride." He instructed
them to watch out for me at all times, in riding, getting
to the location, doing whatever was to be done, and
returning. This was certainly a first! The men were as
stunned as I was. When the skipper left and went
upstairs, the men wanted to know "How come?" I told
them exactly what the skipper had said to me. They
couldn't believe it, but had heard it from the captain, and
then there was much talk about it. One must know at
this time that the captain of a company was the Lord and
Master - he was in supreme command - never to have his
word challenged! I knew for sure that Captain Casey
had taken one hell of a big chance having me ride and
then being "on the line!"

There was no way on earth that the chief was going to find that out! Many years later, I emulated "Captain Mike" when I was a company officer, by allowing a well chosen buff to ride with me.

While still at the fire we broke and drained the hose line and put it back on the apparatus, coupled up. I learned that was done just in case (which has happened) a fire was encountered while returning to quarters, to insure being "on the ready."

The firemen were slapping me on the back congratulating me, and shaking hands with me, praising me for my performance. When we went back in service later at quarters, the captain himself said he was very pleased with me, and I thanked him for the privilege. Before he went to his office to write his report, he said to me, "You were great - I'm sure some day you'll make the job, but more than that, I'll predict you'll be an officer! I hope I'm around to see it."

CHAPTER THREE

"THANKS, MOM"

When I was twenty years old, I learned there was a fireman's test in the making, but the date was unknown. The requirements at that time were that an applicant had to be twenty-one years of age on or before the date of the written test. The men who were studying for promotion at Engine 240 were very giving of their time and knowledge to me - they knew I wanted the job - and they never minded my asking questions. There was though, one big obstacle for me: I would not be twenty-one years of age until July 10th, and that was eight months away; it surely appeared I wouldn't make the eligibility. One of the firemen (who later became a captain) suggested that I go to Delahanty Civil Service School and sign up for their course. He thought the test might be held during the summer, when the schools would be closed.

I took the subway to 14th Street, and for quite a while I stood in front of Delahanty Institute on 15th Street before I cautiously went inside. I was excited as I came full circle with the realization - this was the first step towards my goal - what was going to happen? The first thing I saw was a large counter, the full size of the width of the room. There were many men clerks standing behind it, with applicants in front being waited on. When one of the clerks was free, I was beckoned to him, and he asked what could he do for me. I told him I wanted to sign up for the coming fireman's exam, and the very first question he asked me was my age! I was nervous being asked that, and very timidly I answered, "twenty." He replied that as I was eight months away from the age eligibility I probably would not be eligible. It was his opinion that the test would be held within six months, and he would not enroll me for the course.

I was bitterly disappointed as I left there, and took the long ride home to Brooklyn, thinking how I failed to fulfill my dream. I went back to Engine 240 and explained to my mentor what had happened. He listened to what I said, and remained silent for a few minutes, thinking it all over. He realized how disappointed I was, and he finally said, "Do you remember the clerk who told you that?" I said, "I'd never forget him!" "All right then," he said, "go back there again and speak to a different clerk, not the one who turned you down." A straw looks like a lifeboat to a drowning person, and sad and blue as I was, I envisioned that "straw" as a hope. I went back the next day full of new enthusiasm!

I went over the whole thing in my head as I rode the subway, and came up with a way to avoid the clerk who had turned me down. Finally I was outside Delahanty's, standing by the entrance door, observing all of the clerks behind the large counter; when I was sure I saw the one I had to avoid, I went inside. My plan was to see him engage in conversation with an applicant, and when he did, I went to another clerk who was free, at the far end of the counter. I told him I wanted to enroll for the fireman's course, and the first thing he said to me was, "How old are you?" My spirits immediately collapsed. I had visions of the same thing happening to me again! He was silent, considering my answer. He finally told me he could not assure me the date of the test - it was unknown - but estimated it would be held in the summer time.

Inasmuch as I was eight months away from being eligible, he would enroll me with the provision that if I wasn't eligible, i.e., if the test was held before I was twenty-one (on July 10) he would credit my tuition to the next course for patrolman. I agreed immediately, and signed up. After the necessary paper work was finished and I paid a deposit, I thanked the clerk for his kindness to me, and quickly left the premises to hurry back to Engine 240, and thank my good friend for his advice.

I had signed up for the course on November 23, 1929 for $50.00, and classes began two days later. I still have the enrollment receipt, which states, "If too young, to be credited to patrolman." My emotions ran high - the race against the calendar began - fate and destiny at work again.

I attended classes regularly for both the written and the physical. It was a pleasure, as it was a complete reversal to me from my younger school days. I was in school again because I wanted to be there; what a difference a motive makes! I studied everything given to us at school, and took all the "trial exams," which were made up of a review of all the material given. The gym classes were difficult at the beginning, and we were given the various parts of the physical test step by step. After months of gym work I progressed rapidly, and knew I was ready for the physical. My academic work was going along fine, and the results of the trial exams I had taken were very promising, as I had passed each one. So far so good; I was very pleased with myself.

There is a New York City Newspaper called *The Chief* which is published weekly. It gives up to the minute data on civil service jobs, applications, and filing dates for exams. Eligibility lists are published when released by the Civil Service Commission. No interested candidate seeking a civil service position would ever be without their issue of *The Chief.*

Every Friday evening the paper would be on the newsstand, and I'd be there anxiously waiting for it to arrive. As each issue came out, and the less was said about filing and dates, the better it was for me. One night in January there was a page one article that stated the Civil Service Commission anticipated the filing for the fireman's test would be in February, and the test would probably be held late in June, or early July - dates were not decided upon at the time. I was again filled with excitement, as this was good news and bad news for me. When "early July" raced through my head - if indeed it would be July - would it be before or after July 10th? The timing was critical - this was a cliffhanger for me - my apprehension grew greater and greater while time slowly passed and I eagerly waited for each Friday's edition. Finally, one night the news came! *The Chief* stated the filing would be in February, and due to an estimate of 10,000 filing, there would be four dates for the written exam - July 15, 16, 17, 18! The race against the calendar was over - I had won out - I would be five days over twenty-one!

My cup runneth over with joy! The 10,000 figure seemed staggering; if 1,000 were to be appointed in four years, the odds were ten to one for me to get the job. The incentive was there - I would give it everything I had, and then some to win.

I thanked my mother for having me on July 10th, and not a week or two later. She told me I was expected on my father's birthday, July 21st! Destiny, fate and timing were on my side for sure!

When the dates were published for giving out the

applications early in February, I was there the first day. I filled it out and filed it that day, as it was stated "ties" were broken by application number. As expected, over 10,000 filed, and I was number 417.

I received my notice to report for the test on July 15th, the first day of the exam; it was held at the old opera house on East 68th Street, New York City, where thousands of us showed up. We went through all the necessary steps - fingerprinting, signing papers, etc. - and were seated. The proctors issued instructions and placed the first part of the test face down on our desks. There were three parts to the written test: (1) Memory, (2) Arithmetic, (3) Government. The final of all was called the "Mental," and later, those who passed would be called for the medical and physical tests. As each part of the written test was given, papers were collected at the end, and the next part given, until all three parts were finished.

When it was over and the crowds left the building, there was much talk among the applicants comparing answers. I thought I had done fairly well in all parts - my schooling and preparations paid off - as proven in "The Result of Examination Notice," which was mailed out April 24, 1931. My final average was 90.20, viz: Part I- Memory: 100; Part 2 - Arithmetic: 95; Part 3 - Government: 94; Mental: 95.40; Physical - 85 - passed, and placed on the list: #169. The eligible list for fireman had 3,993 men on it. 4,848 took the Mental Examination, 855 failed - positive proof that preparation is absolutely necessary.

Those who passed the written test were called back for the medical and physical parts of the exam. The medical was a complete going over of our conditions.

FDNY Probationary Class 1932. Ed Schneider is 2nd row from the top, 2nd from the left. Of the 28 young men pictured, six of them were destined to become chiefs.

Those who passed the medical were then called for the physical, which consisted of ten performances in strength. It was obvious that if a candidate did not prepare with gym training, it would have been very difficult to get a decent passing mark. My gym training paid off, as I received 85%.

When all the testing parts were over, I'd report to my mentors at Engine 240, and they estimated that I had about a 90%. They were elated at my good showing.

The Great Depression was with us - there wasn't any work - men were idle and more and more were losing their jobs. One of the men buffs at Engine 240 had gotten me a job as a surety investigator, but before long we were both laid off. Many sold apples on street corners, and the song "Brother Can You Spare A Dime" was written. It has always been remembered as a grim reminder of the depression.

I sold ice cream bricks and eskimo pies during the hot summer, and did my buffing at night. As I was now 21 years old, I applied for and passed the hack drivers test, and drove a cab. Thousands of us us would cruise, or sit and wait at a corner for a fare. A cab ride was a luxury, affordable for those working. Many a day would go by, from 6 A.M. to 4 P.M, when I would make only a couple of dollars. When the fleet owner saw your receipts were almost nothing at the end of the day, he'd say, "Take a vacation!" Then you'd have to find another fleet and shape for a day's work. it wasn't easy!

The months passed slowly, and then came the night of April 18, 1931. The headline in *The Chief* read: "3,993 ON LIST FOR FIREMAN." With the paper in my hand, standing alone by a lighted window, I started looking for my name. The placing began with 96% - I quickly went through the 90's - there was my name - No. 169 - 90.20%! I had beaten the calendar - I had made it! Thanks Mom, for having me on July 10th! Now - on to the unknown - Excellsior!!

CHAPTER FOUR

BAPTISM
BY FIRE

After a practically sleepless Christmas Eve, I proudly reported in to Engine 220 at 8:30 A.M. on Christmas Day, 1931, and became a "probie." On this first day of my 34 year career with the New York City Fire Department, I was on an emotional high. The events leading to my actually getting on the fire department had came full circle.

When one enters a firehouse, he will see a desk on the side of the house, up front near the entrance door. This is the housewatch desk, and is manned by the fireman performing housewatch duty. This duty corresponds in function to guard duty in the military, and is an extremely important part of daily operations. The duty list is prepared by the officer, and a watch is for three hours. Duties include answering the phone, the receipt of alarms, and logging all activities in the company journal. If a civilian enters and reports a fire, the housewatchman has to sound the alarm bell throughout the house, alerting everyone. If a verbally reported fire, the officer on duty takes it from there with prescribed regulations.

There I stood, in front of the housewatch; I gave him my name, and he welcomed me to the job. He directed me to report to the captain's office on the second floor. I knocked, and a voice said, "Come in." I entered and identified myself, and the captain took my personnel information for his records, and then had me go downstairs to the desk and stand roll call. The captain's name was Miller; he was an aloof type - he didn't impress me as being a warm kind man. He assigned me to the night tour - 6 P.M. to 9 A.M. which was the 15 hour tour. In those years we worked the two platoon system. I went home for the intervening nine hours, and returned that evening at 6 P.M. Each unit had two officers - a captain and a lieutenant. The day tour was 9 A.M. to 6 P.M.

One of the men going off at 6 P.M. loaned me his helmet, boots and coat, until I could purchase my own. We became very good friends, and when we worked the same tour, he'd always be watching out for me. Years later we were promoted to lieutenant on the same day, and assigned to nearby units. Sad to relate, he fell six floors from a roof, and died from his injuries. It was a personal loss. He "broke" me in.

I didn't tell anyone I was a buff, and was not going to be looked upon as a "Smart Alec," by letting anyone know what little I knew about the job, and I mean little! I knew some tools and appliances and hose fittings, and I was eager to learn. Some men were helpful, but the real old timers stayed by themselves - no time for the probie. After supper with the men, there followed a lot of good natured kidding, much of it directed at me.

I was told to stay at the watch desk where I would be introduced to the alarms, telephone, etc. - learn the system of bells. In brief, when an alarm box was pulled on a street corner for a fire, a code wheel with cutouts of the number of the box was activated, sending the alarm into the communication headquarters; each borough had its own. The dispatchers receive it, and they transmit to the fire houses via a system of bells, using taps and spaces.

That's the way it used to be. Today there are no more bells; alarm notification to respond is given by dispatchers via computers.

It didn't take too long after I was with the housewatchman the first night on the job to get my first run as a real fireman. I had my gear on in an instant, and away we went, first due, four blocks to the box. It was only "food on the stove." It was a great feeling, like the time I rode with Captain Casey. Upon arrival at the scene, and getting off the engine, my instructions were to stay with the officer. After doing what had to be done - put the pot of burned food in the sink and open windows, we were ordered to return to quarters.

It was at that incident that I first met the man who was to become my idol and inspiration, namely: Captain Thomas J. Lyons, Hook and Ladder 122.

Engine 220 was in a house by itself, and Ladder 122 was the adjoining company. There was a dividing wall between the units which separated them.

Captain Lyons shook my hand, offered his congratulations on my appointment, and warmly put his hand on my shoulder as he spoke to me. This greatly impressed me, as my own two company officers didn't react that way. I found out soon enough that Captain Lyons and my own officers were as far apart as night and day.

That night tour and the next passed without any more runs. I was given a locker, and started my orientation to the job. The captain was an aloof sort and pompous as far as I was concerned; he barely, if ever, spoke to me, the lowly probie. The lieutenant was a grouch - he never spoke to me - and I never knew why he disliked me. Most of my tours were with the lieutenant, and sensing as I had that he disliked me from the start, I couldn't warm up to him.

Battalion Chiefs Ward and Cooney were in our quarters on the third floor. They were fine men, well-liked, stayed upstairs and didn't bother anyone. At chow time we'd all be together in the kitchen, and I'd be the listener, while the others talked.

Chief Cooney and I became very friendly; he was as fine a man as I ever met. He enjoyed telling me stories of his coming to the U.S.A., from Ireland - especially being lost at Ellis Island. He told me of his searching for the man who was to look after him in the U.S.A. Finally he found him in downtown Brooklyn on Pacific Street. It was a beautiful story - the man turned out to be Ned Brannigan, who turned out to be my wife's grandfather!

I got along fine with all the men in the company except one. He was arrogant, a know-it-all, and a loud mouth. He clearly was the firehouse lawyer, and a disturber. His type can usually be found in the job in any unit: the one who had seniority, and usually was a "pet" of the officers. The old-timers wouldn't take his guff, nor his disturbing ways; but in me, the new man (probie) he was having a field day. The day came when I knew enough was too much with him and it took place at a "worker" - a residence fire in a dwelling, with two rooms involved with fire upon our arrival, first due. As we stretched our hose line to the fire building, then removed enough to take us into the fire, the next move was to uncouple the hose and put the nozzle on the male end, start the water, and advance into the fire. I had the nozzle and was connecting it to the hose when "big mouth" demanded I give him the nozzle. I held onto it, and words started to fly between us. I told him if he didn't back off, the only way he'd get the nozzle was when I'd shove it up his rear!

Chief Cooney saw the whole thing and admired the action. We got water in the line and kept advancing into the fire, heat, and smoke. It was nothing unusual - another "worker," another job - a routine house fire. With the fire extinguished and all necessary work finished, we were ordered back to quarters and started picking up our hose. "Big Mouth" started at me again, and then I told him, "I've had all of your bully way I'm going to take from you, and when we get back to quarters, it's you and me into the cellar and the winner comes up!"

Our job was completed at quarters, and Big Mouth was at me again. The lieutenant had gone to his office to do his paper work of the fire. Here was the moment of truth for me - I invited him into the cellar to have it out - no holds barred - and the loser doesn't open his mouth to the lieutenant about the fight!

He backed down like the bully that he was; he refused my offer to settle the bad blood between us and whatever it was he had against me. I gave him the offer again, in heated words, with the men standing there taking it all in. He tried to talk me out of the fight, refusing the offer. I really tore into him verbally, letting him know he had better stop his bullyness with me from here on in. I wasn't afraid to take him on - I had some experience with a buddy of mine who was a boxer; and I sparred with him, and I knew I could take care of myself.

That incident set me up fine with the brothers who had witnessed it all. Those who didn't see it heard about it, and it was common knowledge that the bully caved in to the probie! The men liked what thy saw and had heard from me, and they enjoyed taunting Big Mouth for backing down. From there on I had no more trouble with him.

Many years later we met on the street - I was then a chief, and he was still in the job on the fire boat fleet as a marine engineer. It was a tense moment, but I soon realized he had mellowed; we didn't bring up the past - either one of us - we had a few minutes chat, about himself, mostly on the boats, and of me being a chief. Arriverderci!

Captain Lyons lived in Flatbush, and after work would walk home via Prospect Park. I lived at the other end of the park, and we used to walk together to Park Circle. He was the skipper next door (Ladder 122) and oh how I wished I had been sent to his unit! He was a man among men, tall, of great character, a wonderful family man, and had the reputation of a great fire fighter. For all his greatness, whenever his name was brought up, you would always hear about his being a fine human being. We became great friends, and I learned a lot from him as we walked home in the park. That was the beginning of our relationship - him giving me sound advice about "getting in the books." He had wisdom seldom found in people - clearly he was able to understand the difference between "people" and "things," and that I believe was his greatest asset.

Years later when I had left Engine 220 and was at Ladder 148, Captain Lyons selected me as his aide when he was promoted to Battalion Chief. What an honor that was for me - selecting me, of all the ones he knew, and those who would have given anything to be his aide!

That's how it all began - I now had some six years in the job - five of my best at Ladder 148. It was with a sad heart that I left such wonderful men and officers, to go with the man I idolized to be his aide.

It is well stated that history cannot be truly written until the years have passed: how true! I sure found out about the incompetency of the lieutenant of my first year in the job when I was a "know nothing probie," as the years passed on. I was advancing in rank, gaining experience in different operations, plus years and years of civil service schools and "in the books."

Here's an instance of his incompetency - remember, I can say this now, not then - he was dead wrong in failing to take the proper action, and lucky to get away with it. Inadvertently, as you will note, I had something to do with the result by doing what I did.

I was walking down the street, about a half block from the firehouse, on my way to the 6 P.M.-9 A.M. tour; it was 5:30 P.M., and I saw the lieutenant standing in front of quarters looking up the street. He had a 2-1/2 gallon soda and acid extinguisher on the sidewalk. He saw me approaching, and hollered in a very loud voice to hurry up. I double-timed it to a run, not having the slightest idea what he wanted. When I got to him I found out he was yelling at me to take the extinguisher to 12th Street near 5th Avenue, and gave me the house number. He said a civilian had reported to quarters that there was smoke in his house! From the firehouse on 11th Street, between 7th and 8th Avenues, to 12th Street and 5th Avenue, is just about four blocks away.

I did what I was told, and lugged the "can" the four blocks - believe it or not. The lieutenant should have responded with his company to a verbal alarm, as provided for in the regulations. I arrived at the address and saw a crowd of people in front of the house, a two-story frame dwelling with smoke coming from many parts of the house. I knew this couldn't be handled by me alone without any tools - just a "can" (extinguisher) so I immediately told a man to pull the fire box on the corner, which he did.

I entered the house to do what I could do, but I couldn't see fire - only smoke. I inquired if anyone was in the house, but no one knew. I went down to the cellar as the smoke was heaviest from there. The apparatus came within minutes, and I apprised the lieutenant of conditions. It developed that the fire originated in the cellar, and fire was in the walls and ceiling. It wouldn't have taken but a few minutes, and the fire would be into the floor above, on its way up!

The truckmen opened up the ceiling and walls, exposing the fire, and it was extinguished. When Captain Lyons heard about this, he couldn't believe it; he asked the lieutenant about it face to face as I stood by. It was one of the few times in my long association with him that I ever heard him blast the lieutenant for not taking the proper action and responding instead of sending me to run four blocks away with a can. It is not difficult to imagine the fire spreading into the walls and gaining headway. It also developed that there was an occupant asleep upstairs in a room, unbeknownst to the man who reported the "smell of smoke" to the fire house four blocks away! All the elements of a possible loss of life were present and possible.

Captain Lyons had a great reputation, and was a fantastic fire officer who knew his business. The lieutenant was just the opposite.

I was just off probationary period of three months when one day we responded first due, to a fire which developed into four alarms. During those four months I had been to a five alarm church fire, many small bedroom fires, some commercial fires, and one very bad two alarm cellar fire in a furniture factory. I was comfortable in all the fires I had worked at, and gained more and more confidence as time went on.

When we arrived at the location of this to be four alarm fire, all of us knew instantly we were in for a tough job. The building was a one-story chemical factory, about 75' wide, and lengthwise ran from one block to the next, about 150 feet in depth. We quickly had our hose line stretched to a doorway entrance, got water in the hose, and entered. Many times over the years I looked back at our situation and realized the severity and intensity of the fire on arrival, and what should have been done. Our orders were to advance into the fire with our hose line. Our chief had sized up the seriousness of the fire and had ordered a second alarm right away; this was later followed by superior arriving chiefs, to the transmittal of the third and fourth alarms.

We advanced our hose about 20 to 25 feet into the building, crouched down, facing a bad heat and smoke condition rushing at us as we poured water ahead of us. It was only about two minutes at best driving our stream ahead of us, when the fire caused our water to be thrown back into our faces - and it was red hot water - not the cold water we were getting out of the nozzle! All of us were huddled together - four of us, and our lieutenant, - instantly from the hot water coming at us with great force, we were then in a room full of fire - no longer just heat and smoke, but fire all over us! All of us scrambled on our stomachs for the door, the way we had come in, by

Three of the four men from Engine 220 who were caught in a backdraft, recovering in the hospital. Left, Ed Schneider; center, J. Quigg; right A. Olson. Not pictured, F. Donovan.

following our dropped hose line. The factory door opened outwardly - we reached the door and fell out into the street. I was at the nozzle with another man by my side, and all I could recall was being grabbed by the neck of my coat and yanked out, about five feet from the street. My helmet was knocked off my head, and all of us landed in the street, badly burned on the face and hands. The lieutenant shielded his face and hands, and he only received a slight burn on one ear. The four of us linemen were badly burned.

We were taken to a nearby coffee pot restaurant, where we were treated and removed to a hospital via ambulance. This was real scary, as the restaurant had mirrors all over its walls, and we looked at ourselves in those mirrors and couldn't believe what we were looking at! We had been caught in a dreaded backdraft - a phenomenon of superheated smoke and gases which had ignited.

The four of us were put in one hospital room, and we could see each other's burns - we didn't know what the end result would be. There was talk going on by the doctors and nurses, and we had heard "whispers" of maybe we had inhaled flame into our throats and nostrils - and if that was the case, then we were in bad trouble. As it turned out, we didn't - we were burned, but all of us healed up in time and recovered. That was my baptism by fire - four months on the job!

CHAPTER FIVE

"I'M NOT THROUGH WITH YOU YET!"

Captain Lyons was not at the fire, but heard what had happened. On our walks home through the park after work, he explained what a backdraft was, and how it happened. Here was a great man, telling me, the rookie, that the skylights on the roof should have been pulled off for the building to be ventilated, thus allowing the heat, smoke, fire and gases to be released to the outer air.

I want to stress at this time that I never made a practice of "second guessing" any fire operations that I had not operated at. The easiest thing in life is to criticize someone, particularly after a critique of an unusual fire. Many times a few of us while studying for the chief's test would make our own judgments as to merits and perhaps faults, but only in retrospect, doing a survey of past events. The chiefs at any fire are the ones responsible for their actions - not those of us who weren't there. Suffice to say, "I don't know - I wasn't there."

The four stages in controlling any fire after determining the location and extent of fire, are (1) to confine the fire to the area found upon arrival and prevent its spread; (2) to attack it quickly with effective hose streams, either by attack or defense, or both; (3) advance hose lines to the seat of the fire and extinguish it; (4) the overhauling stage which consists of a thorough examination, seeking any fire in concealed or hidden places.

The whole field of studying firefighting and fire prevention consists of many facets: such include chemistry, physics, hydraulics, laws, ordinances, building construction, apparatus, fire strategy, etc. The list of subjects is almost endless. It takes years of studying and much time and effort. The saying "knowledge is power," surely fits. As students well know, we can never learn enough, and are constantly learning to improve our efficiency and professionalism, and to become aware of increasing our competency in operations and performance.

In order to prevent the same men from always working together, at the end of each fourth week, the rules stated that one man from each of the two platoons would change over to the other's platoon. There was favoritism in this arrangement, as I soon found out. As a Sunday off for me was coming up, I'd be swung over to the other platoon, thus losing any Sundays off, plus adding more working hours for one, (the changeover) and less hours for the other one who changed. This went on month after month - I was the one to "change over," while one of the lieutenant's favorites would get my Sunday. My friends would confide in me, telling me I was getting a bad deal; I was young, single, and keeping company with my wife to be, and we looked forward to being together on a Sunday. I kept all of this to myself. I was a "rookie" - I did not complain - but you can bet it did not go unnoticed. If there were any details given out such as messenger, funeral, theatre detail, or a thirty-day assignment to another unit, I would get it.

I welcomed the change to other units for a thirty-day detail, and when the month was up, I'd ask that captain to please keep me there for another month. I would meet other officers and new men, and recognized how good it felt to be treated fairly. One thing in particular really annoyed me, and that was being the messenger with a fire report (hand delivered) to a far off battalion, if we had a run through the night. The practice was for the messenger to deliver the fire report, and "keep on going," meaning he didn't have to come back to the firehouse for the 9 A.M. roll call. I'd get the messenger duty, go by trolley to a far off place of delivery, and then have to be back as I was told by the lieutenant. I'd just about get back by five or ten minutes. There was no way out of this - there he'd be, smirking at knowing he had made me come back, and he knew anyone else could have gone home. That was a real hurt that was impossible to endure - the price of favoritism!

One of my friends at Engine 240 asked me if I'd like a copy of the order of my appointment. Of course I said yes - that was a very nice favor, a memento to keep over the years. He requested his friend in headquarters to send it to me; he sent it in an envelope, addressed to Engine 220. Later I was asked if I received it, and why I didn't thank my friend for sending it to me. When I told him that I never got it, he inquired by contacting the lieutenant who received it. It was addressed to Engine 220 and not to me; therefore it was not given to me. My friend told his contact, and he said he couldn't believe it - it was for me - not Engine 220. Upon learning that, he then sent the order in a sealed envelope addressed to me, c/o Engine 220. When the lieutenant received it, he fumed. He recognized the script writing, (the one who sent it had a script handwriting - an absolutely unmistakable beautiful writing to look at) knowing what it was. He grudgingly gave it to me, and I still have it among my mementos.

All of these happenings are told in depth because I

want the reader to know how my spirit was being broken by this lieutenant - so much and more - that I had reached the breaking point with it all. I considered resigning from the job - my dream was shattered! I could not bear the thought of all that I had worked so hard for to get was only an illusion - a false impression and not a reality. I could not accept the unjust treatment. It was different being on the inside looking out, than on the outside looking in! He almost succeeded in crushing me; I couldn't fight or argue - I was certainly in a "Catch 22" position - between a rock and a hard place.

So that's how things were for me. I did my house-cleaning chores, did my fire duty, and I tried my best at all times. I was never late - always early - and never got a calling down for not doing my job; the fat was in the fire.

On a day off I went to my mentor at Engine 240, where I had buffed, and told him my troubles. I said I knew of no way out of my situation and was seriously thinking about resigning after one year on the job. He was flabbergasted at what I told him, but was long enough on the job to listen and hear me out - and understand. He had known me for years, and was with me on the run that Captain Casey allowed me to ride with him. He knew how much I wanted the job. This was the man, who himself became a captain later on, who had told me (as related earlier) some day I'd be a chief. Our relationship was the best.

Once more he came to my rescue. He said the way out for me was to be transferred. Transferred? Me get transferred? There was no such thing in those days (as it is now) of submitting an application for a transfer to another unit. It had to be done politically, or by contact with headquarters, and I only had one year on the job.

On a walk home through the park one morning I told Captain Lyons my feelings, and he understood perfectly. It so happened that Fireman Vince Kane had served under Captain Lyons, and Vince was now president of the U.F.A. They too were great friends. When the captain said he would intercede for me through Vince, he asked me where I would like to be transferred. Imagine that! A choice! I told him "get me out of Engine 220 - never mind the choice!" He explained a unit would have to be specified. I let him know that some of the men I was appointed with were at Ladder 148, and they said it was a great outfit. He put the "contract" in for me through Vince for Ladder 148. I was transferred there within a week, on the very next order!

The lieutenant was furious when the orders were published. I knocked on his door for permission to enter; he sneered at me in his usual grouchy manner, and arrogantly growled, "You looked for the transfer, didn't you?" I said, "Yes Sir." His answer was, "I don't care where you go, I'm not through with you yet!" I've never forgotten his words - I knew I wasn't going to have a confrontation with him, or an argument. I was sure he'd charge me with disrespect and/or insubordination, so I did not answer him. I knew I was out of that unit, and I was secure and in control of myself. I turned in my property to him - spanner and hose strap - and left his office. I said so long to the guys; I had made many good friends there, and they wished me the best. One of the men was a prime mover in breaking me in when I was sent there, and he had introduced me to the girl I married. One was promoted to lieutenant the day I was made lieutenant. Another served as my lieutenant when I was a chief. There was a lot of emotion shown when I walked out of those quarters. I felt life was about to begin for me - I was happy to be on my way to a new start. What a beautiful feeling it was when I walked away from Engine 220. It was a new beginning!

CHAPTER SIX

A NEW BEGINNING

I reported to Ladder 148 the next day at 9 A.M. as per the transfer order, and was assigned to the 6 to 9 tour that night. I met the officer on duty, Lieutenant Whalen, and gave him the needed personnel information for his records. We had a small chat - he saw I only had one year on the job - and he welcomed me to the company.

Ladder 148 was in quarters with Engine 282 located in Boro Park on 12th Avenue and 42nd Street. It was primarily a residential area of apartment houses, stores and three-story frame houses of "balloon construction," called Queen Anns, peculiar to the area. It didn't take long for my indoctrination to the Queen Ann - I did not have any fires in them in Park Slope, and Boro Park was heavily populated with that type of residence. The officers and men were very experienced in those type of fires, which had peculiarities in construction. A fire, usually starting in a cellar, may gain headway before its discovery and the transmission of an alarm, causing a high probability of fire extending upwards via interior walls which were open all the way up to the attic at the top. The space between the outer clapboards of the house and the inside walls could easily be a foot wide, presenting a fast upward spread of fire to the upper floors and attic.

These were difficult fires to attack - the truckmen had to pull ceilings and walls, and the engine company chased the fire as it traveled. The attic was the most difficult to get at, as there was only a very narrow stairway leading to it, which was usually filled with storage of all kinds. Roof ventilation was imperative to advance a hoseline up the stairs and into the attic - much punishment was taken by the men gaining their way up. The potential of spread was recognized by the chiefs and officers working at these fires, and they had become very efficient and competent in operations and performance. This is also true of other parts of the city, where problems are peculiar to the area, such at Staten Island with the bad brush fire situations, Manhattan areas of high buildings, old law tenements, loft buildings, factories, etc. Then there is the waterfront with ships and pier fires. Queens has many residences and taxpayers, as has the Bronx. Each geographical part of the five boroughs indicates the kind of fires, hazards, risks and perils particular to the sections of the city. Men working in an area for a long time can really be called "specialists" in their fire neighborhoods - knowing, understanding, and doing their jobs expertly.

Now I was in a house with two units, a ladder and an engine company - usually twelve men and the officers - a house full of great guys, good decent officers - who could ask for more? I was easily and readily accepted by everyone, plus I knew some who were appointed with me. The very first tour of duty, my first night tour, only a half hour elapsed before we went out to a hard working "all hands" bad fire, in a large store, first due. I was assigned to a six foot hook, and told to stay with Lieutenant Whalen. We pulled metal tin ceilings, and it was hard work - a big change going from engine work with the hoseline to truck work. I was working the best I could, with blisters on my fingers, but it was a good feeling of accomplishment and satisfaction - here I was happy.

After our return to quarters, I was busy with the rest of the guys cleaning the tools and washing the wheels of our truck. Lieutenant Whelan came over to me, placed his arm over my shoulder almost like a father and told me he was pleased with my work. He said I had performed just fine, and he was glad to have me in the company. The lieutenant was a great firefighter who knew his job; in his younger days he had been a chief's aide, and he was respected by his men and his superiors. He was a kind man, considerate and conscientious; he loved to tell us youngsters tales of the old days, and we loved to listen to them. When he retired we gave him one great big party in a ballroom filled to capacity; it was a pleasure and a privilege to have served under him. The accolades flowed by all speakers at this party - everyone admired him - the best judgment of all was the love he had by his men and his peers.

These two companies, Engine 282 and Ladder 148 had a great reputation for firefighting and men being promoted to officers. Our other lieutenant was Frank Carney, a giant of a man, ex-navy and one hell of a firefighter. He was a fine, decent, kind man, with a great sense of humor, always enjoying a laugh. I had the greatest regard for my lieutenants, and became greatly attached to them. Our company was without a captain, as the engine company had one. That vacancy was filled much later, and again we were favored with good skippers. The engine captain was Captain Ed McCormack who was overseer of both units. How could guys be so fortunate, having such good officers? Captain Ed was a great guy - a hard hitter, ex-fighter in his day, name of Eddie Kid Mac. He was just as well liked by us in the truck company as our lieutenants were. All of the officers were good men who knew their jobs and were held in high regard.

Yes siree - this was going from night to day for me. I loved every tour of my five years there, and it was real hard on me leaving there to become aide to Chief Lyons. When you love what you do, and are exhilarated with cheer, happiness and contentment, it's as Jackie Gleason used to say - "How Sweet It Is"! Years later my Lieutenant Carney and I became chiefs, and worked together in the same battalion - what a great reunion - what a swell guy!

As I said in the foreword to these tales, it was a great pleasure serving under fine, decent men, but there were others who were just the opposite. This seems the time to relate an "opposite" story. In Engine 282 we had a fine young man appointed there, well liked by all, and an excellent firefighter, name of Tom O'Neil. He was strong, well built, young and handsome. He had been a speed typist, and knew shorthand. Captain McCormack had been transferred out of our unit and his replacement was a captain who made Captain Bligh look like a saint. His reputation well preceded him - he was a tough disciplinarian - mean and nasty, and enjoyed finding faults and preferring charges against the men for any reason he could find. There were many of us "in the books," so when we saw what he was, we would avoid him by not associating with him.

Poor Tom O'Neil was so disliked by the old grouch inhuman captain that his spirit was slowly but surely being broken. The final instance was one night tour about 6 A.M. when the captain went out into the bunkroom, went to Tom's bed, pulled the covers off him, and growled at him, "Get up O'Neil, and go out on hydrant inspections!" This was only one of his despicable moves - he was hated by all, lieutenants and men.

There are incidents of his nastiness that would fill a book - suffice to say he was a tyrant. Tom went out as ordered. He was a rookie, and we suffered with him, as he truly was one fine young man. The next day when we left quarters, I told him my story of unhappiness as a rookie, and advised him to get away from the skunk and seek a transfer - that was what I did, and he was in a lot more hot water than I was in! He was really impressed at what I told him, as he had no idea our situations were similar. I persuaded him to get a transfer before he "broke," and through friends he got transferred. As the years went by and I was a chief, he became a captain. I'd make it a point to visit him at his quarters often; you have no idea how he would greet me and actually hug me with joy when we'd meet. This fine specimen of manhood got sick and died young. Rest in peace, Tom.

Our Lieutenant Carney told us a story of when he was on the list for promotion to lieutenant; he had worked under one of the most overbearing lieutenants on the job. They had a new man on the job, who came over from the police department. He was tall and husky and made a good truckman and was well liked by the men. He suffered under the tyrant to the end that he told the men, including Frank Carney, that he was disillusioned about the Fire Department and was going back to the Police Department. It was only on the insistence of the then Fireman Carney, who was about to have the same rank as lieutenant, that he turned it all around by telling the lieutenant to lay off the man. He was a good man and an asset to the company. This man stayed on our job and the tyrant got off his back, all to the benefit of the fire department. He went on to be a lieutenant, and did a tops-up job in a rescue company. The tyrant carried on his nasty ways as a captain and then chief. He would spare no one his acid tongue and overbearing ways.

It was a case of authority gone to his head. I too ran across him when I was a captain and he was a chief. He was so intent on acting like he was the master of all his subordinates that he went after everyone - me included. The years had made a difference - I became a chief - we both had the same rank now - he couldn't browbeat me then, as he had before. Time and time again when I was acting deputy chief in our division, we'd meet at fires, and he tried to sweet talk me to no end, as if prior years of being a tyrant didn't exist. I was never again intimidated by him. He did such dirty things to the men, I tell you he was in a class almost by himself, but there were others as bad as he was. Surely in their cases, it was a case of rank going to their heads, behaving like dictators. That's why it was such a pleasure to work with officers who were human beings. We were thankful for the many "good guys" on the job.

I have given these examples of the meanness of some officers in those days to relate to the reader that all was not "milk and honey;" there are many more that could be told. The point is, thank God those days are gone and replaced by an entire new breed of up and coming officers who are human beings. I'm glad I had a part in it. There's another viewpoint in those early days of being promoted. It may not be nice to say, but many a man's incentive was built on a universal expression, and that was, "If that guy can be an officer, so can I."

CHAPTER SEVEN

"SHENANIGANS"

A lieutenant's exam was held when I was two years on the job. I was enthralled and watched the enthusiasm the students had preparing for the test. With only two years on the job, I was not yet eligible. There were 1,907 who took the test, and 636 passed. Eleven men from our units (282 and 148) passed and were promoted to lieutenant; this was an extremely high percentage. It followed that many men looked for a transfer there - I was fortunate to be there; my group picked up where the ones who passed left off. They were extremely helpful to us and steered us in the right direction by sharing their knowledge with us before they were promoted.

The exams were held every four years. Finally my turn came. Let me give you a quote from the civil service school chief instructor, "The examination was the most difficult ever held for lieutenant. This was conclusively proven by the fact that of the 2,094 Firemen who competed, only 360, or 17% passed." There were five of us in our units who made it. I was a lieutenant! As time went on, of the five, three of us rose to be chiefs. The other two passed away young, both died as captains, never getting to take the chief's test. By the way, one of us five attained a place on the list for the highest rank, chief of department. There were chiefs who were as competent as he, but none more competent. He became a chief in charge of Brooklyn and Queens. We were a closely knit group, always being helpful to the ones who came in after us, as the men before us were helpful to us.

When I married my wife, the off duty men came to our wedding. One had a moving picture camera and recorded it on film, which he later gave to me. Knowing the background of "shenanigans and tricks," I thought I was in for a grand slam from them. Some had "whispered" and it got back to me that perhaps the bride would be kidnapped! I sweat that out, as nothing was impossible with those guys. I believe it was Lieutenants Whelan and Carney who squashed that; then again, it may have been just said so it would get back to me, for me to sweat out. Nothing happened except a lot of tin cans were tied to the car to make a racket. The church was near Engine 220, and as we went past the firehouse they blew their whistles, sirens and bells. It was a nice remembrance from the guys where I had started out in the job.

Engine 220 was smack in the middle of the block, with residences - homes, apartments and families. The neighbors were our friends, and at holiday times they would bring goodies of fine food to us. My wife's family lived on the block all their lives, Mr. & Mrs. Higgins, and their twelve children. The younger boy, my brother-in-law to be, John Higgins, was the buff at Ladder 122 under the command of Captain Lyons. One of the girls, Grace, used to enter quarters when Ladder 122 was out, and she'd slide the fire house sliding pole with the other kids. She and Captain Lyons would love to tell how he caught them in the act one day, got a hold of Grace and would pretend he was gong to slap her backside, and say to her, "Go home Higgins - stop it before you get hurt." Grace became a nun, and every chance she got, she'd tell the then Chief Lyons that story. He was a religious man with great respect for clergy and nuns - he'd ask her forgiveness - all of us would laugh at that forever! What a man he was! Many a home cooked meal Mrs. Higgins would give to Captain Lyons by her son John. We have many wonderful memories of those days. I often tell my wife Rita, I knew her brother John before I knew her and that he was a "go between" for us.

Back at 282 and 148 things were not so jovial as before when we had Captain McCormack. Lieutenant Carney was on the list for captain, and all of us, including him, were not laughing any more. We were now under the gun of a mean, nasty captain. He tried his best to get Lieutenant Carney provoked into anger and cause him to be insubordinate and disrespectful to him. This would cause charges and really hurt Lieutenant Carney for his being a captain. All of us saw this and knew what the skunk was up to, and we did all we could to calm our lieutenant down and keep him away from the captain. One 9 A.M. roll call as both units were lined up for the "master's" inspection of our badges, books of rules, spanner and ladder straps, Lieutenant Carney saw no humor in what took place and smiled. He was directly in front of me when "Captain Bligh" saw him smiling and said to him, "You - Carney - take that smile off your face, or I'll wipe it off you!" We had our overcoats on, and I reacted immediately by taking a firm grip on his belt on the back of his overcoat, holding him from doing anything. With teeth clenched, I said "No, lieutenant, no." The lieutenant reacted instantly, said nothing, and it was over. That was a real tense five seconds, as both stared at each other. Not a word was spoken by either of them - it could have exploded into a volatile situation with some terrible complications.

One of the most dangerous, vicious and threatening situations developed one evening to one of my good friends. My wife was visiting her mother, and I was home alone when my doorbell rang. I was not expecting anyone, and as I answered the ring, I stood in shock as I opened my door. There stood a good friend from my company "under the influence," feeling high. I told him to come in, and asked him what was going on and what was the occasion for the visit. I put the coffee pot on, and he told me a story that made my hair stand up.

He told me he had gone to the captain's house, rung the bell, and the captain answered. As soon as he opened the door, my friend Mike assaulted him! This was terrible - after the assault and name calling, Mike left and came straight to my home. There were several of us living in the same neighborhood who worked in our company, and Mike chose to come to me. Oh God, what to do? Hours later after talking it out, I felt I had perhaps arrived at a solution, weak as it may be, but to a drowning man a straw looks like a lifeboat. He was sure the captain recognized him in the melee, but it was a dark night, and there was no lighted entrance where it took place. It was a long shot chance, but we agreed that's all we had. I would swear he was with me and my wife at the time, visiting us - deny it - deny it - and deny it, was the way we worked it out, and I tell you it was scary! My wife and I would be his alibi and stick to it. He got sobered up and went home. He promised to be in good condition for the morning - but it sure was a sleepless night.

We reported for duty in the morning, and he looked fine. There we all stood at roll call, and we shivered at what was going to take place. What a relief - nothing was said by the captain - not a word of the incident was spoken by him; no one but Mike and myself shared this secret, and it was never revealed to anyone. Mike and I figured out there wasn't any positive recognition and no proof, so the captain said nothing. Mike was on the next lieutenant's list and was promoted to a New York company. He got married and moved out of our neighborhood; we hardly saw each other over the years, but remained steadfast friends. He died young - our secret was never told until now.

Not long after the incident, the Captain preferred charges against one of the new men, who was on housewatch duty. He had such a diabolical mind, he really outdid himself with this one. His charge against the fireman was that he had pants on which were not officially stamped by the Bureau of Uniform Inspection in accordance with the regulations! The fireman, a nice, clean cut fellow, had bought and used a new pair of pants for the training school; the pants were only a few months old and everyone would have pants like that - they were called "savers" - and were worn on duty at work, keeping the stamped pair in the locker, so as not to spoil them while working at cleaning quarters or at a fire.

When this happened, everyone was furious - nothing like it was ever heard of before or after! This, plus all of the previous goings on, finally reached higher levels. How, who, or whatever it was that brought it about, we never found out. The chiefs knew 282 and 148 were tops in firefighting, had many men on the promotion lists, and were dependable. Morale used to be the greatest, and now it was at low ebb. The "Brass" went to work and scrutinized the company journals, examining all entries, looking for omissions - failures of entries which should have been made - and they found plenty! We heard they had some forty items against the captain, but boiled it down to a certain few. They transferred him out to Harlem! We heard that he never went to work at his new company, but reported sick, and retired from there. I can tell you there was lots of joy over that, and later, when he died, there was little sorrow.

We got a new skipper who was a fine gentleman, liked by everyone. He was a great student and was in the right place with all the other students. He went on to become chief in charge of Brooklyn, and made many friends. I was particularly fond of him - his brother, now an officer - was one of my mentors when I was a buff at Engine 240. They were highly thought of and respected on the job. It was men such as they and others like them, that made it a pleasure for me to serve.

CHAPTER EIGHT

FROM CHIEF'S AIDE TO LIEUTENANT

I knew that if Captain Lyons ever made it to Battalion Chief that he would choose me as his chief's aide.

The new list for battalion chief was soon established, and Captain Lyons placed number one on it! There was such joy and overpowering emotions - it was great just to see him pass with a mark that would be reached for promotion. But placing number one was sheer ecstasy! Talk about "bittersweet" - he was on the previous list for chief, but had not been reached when the list was terminated by its four-year statute of limitations.

He was made acting chief before he was promoted permanently, and was in our battalion. He'd visit our quarters at Ladder 148 and accuse himself of "jinxing" the previous list, because he knew I would be his aide, and he counted the chicken before it hatched. The next examination he said he promised not to take me as his aide, until the list came out. Thus no more "jinx!" He took the disappointment and the joy graciously, just as the great man he was, never allowing the number one spot go to his head, and grateful and appreciative for all congratulations which he received. I was thrilled - I would be his aide!

It wasn't too long before promotions that he became *Chief* Lyons. He submitted my name to be his aide, and

I went with him. We were assigned as relief between the Flatbush area and Park Slope battalions, the latter where he was captain and I was fireman.

My lieutenant list was shortly established, and I was on it in a perfect spot to be promoted in due time. Now I had to learn the duties of an aide, as all I had in experience was engine and ladder work. The aide is considered the "right arm" to the chief, as his duties are many, both in the office (clerical work) and at fires. There is a constant flow of reports coming from the companies, which have to be examined and endorsed as they are passed on to headquarters. There was a spare aide in our quarters who broke me in; he was an excellent teacher and a long time aide to a former chief. This was all new to me, to learn how so much office work was attached to being a chief, as well as an aide. My promotional studies were extremely valuable in the learning process. The aide's job was invaluable to me when I was promoted, giving me a tremendous advantage in assuming officer's rank. At fires the aide would take the chief's orders, give them to incoming responding officers for placements at operations, and gather all needed information at the scene for fire reports, which would be done upon return to quarters. The aide also reported by telephone to communication the particulars of fires. Having good relations with the dispatchers was a "must." I got to know them real well - they were very helpful. I became good friends with many of them.

I will give you an example of how being an aide was such an asset to me when I was a lieutenant. The officer first to arrive at a fire is in command until he is relived by an officer superior in rank. When a street box alarm was transmitted, the response was three engine companies, two ladder companies, and a chief.

It was four A.M. when we responded to what turned out to be a very serious fire. We had a chief in our quarters, and when I turned out, I saw the chief's car was not in quarters. His car was missing from alongside the engine - he was out to another fire, and I knew I'd be in charge, as I was assigned "first due" until relieved by a superior. We could smell, and then observe, much smoke as we were on our way - blocks from the location - and I knew we were going to a "worker." A half block from the scene, straight ahead of us, there was a dwelling with a store front, and the smoke was roaring out of the store at great velocity - heavy, thick, brown and black smoke - it was twisting and rolling as if it was being blown out. I halted the pumper at a hydrant about 150 feet from the store, jumped off, and hopped onto the hose wagon, which had stopped alongside the pumper.

Everyone realized the seriousness of the situation as I ordered two lines of 2-1/2" hose stretched simultaneously, the first one to go into the wagon's deck pipe, and the other for a hand line. The wagon was placed in front of the building, the hose broken and connected to the siamese from the deck pipe. People were standing on the window sills over the store, screaming for help, and threatening to jump out of the windows. Just as we had made our connection, within seconds, the entire store lighted up with fire, replacing the heavy smoke condition with flame. I yelled at the top of my voice to the occupants not to jump - the fastest water I've ever seen obtained came out of the deck pipe, and we swept the front of the premises and the store with this heavy appliance stream.

The men did a tremendous job. The handline was also ready, and I put that into the store. Between both lines, we had attacked a severe fast burning fire and had prevented anyone from jumping. I had ordered the ladder company first in to ladder and rescue work - they were under the command of an acting lieutenant, and did a terrific job getting everyone out - no casualties. The second engine company arrived, led by a lieutenant, and I immediately had him get into operations up the stairs. The third engine came in with a lieutenant in charge, and I ordered him to operate from the rear. The second due ladder company arrived with a lieutenant in charge - all lieutenants!

I put his unit to work at rescue, search and ventilation - all hands working - everyone heavily engaged, and still no chief had arrived. The dispatcher had to special call the next available chief, who incidentally was assigned as the third alarm chief - all others nearest were out!

He had a long trip - all the way from the Red Hook section miles away. The fire was under control when he arrived, and everything taken care of. I was sure glad to see the chief - he and I had been firemen together at Ladder 148 for two years before he was promoted to lieutenant from there. He was one of the top students, and remarked how all my good training from there had paid off. I told him not to forget that I was aide to Chief Lyons and that was the prime factor; he fully agreed. As each unit was dismissed by the chief as no longer needed, I got much praise by all those lieutenants, and I sure patted them and their companies on the back for a job "well done." When the chief dismissed me for our return to quarters, I thanked him and said I was glad to see him again, in more ways than one - he understood! I had the highest praise for my men - they were all great - it was a job where everything "clicked." I had a wonderful feeling of satisfaction - even though the next day I couldn't talk - I had strained my vocal chords and couldn't speak for hours later!

A year later Chief Lyons and I were transferred from the relieving group to a steady assignment in downtown Brooklyn. I was a full-fledged aide by then, and the chief and I were a smooth working team. He was very pleased with my work and how efficient I had become, and I was happy as I could be.

The time was drawing near for my promotion to lieutenant and knowing I would soon be leaving my idol wasn't easy, notwithstanding the fact that I was on my way up in the department. I realized it was another chapter in my life, and a challenge as to what was ahead.

The 1938 World's Fair opening was rapidly approaching, and the fire department had been making plans to insure the safety of the anticipated millions of visitors. One concern was the itinerants who would be staying in rooming and guest homes. The next group of firemen who were to be promoted to lieutenant were assigned to Fire Prevention, augmenting their inspectional forces. I was in that category, and was detailed from Chief Lyons to what was called the Central Building Inspection Squad, until we were promoted. The squad was under the command of Captain Adams, a very good friend of Chief Lyons and me, whom I had met while we were working in Flatbush. We reported as directed, and Captain Adams gave us our instructions. He designated me as the group's leader in the organizing, supervising and layout of the inspections.

This was my first introduction to leadership. Our assignment was to inspect rooming and guest homes in the area of the fair, and at times to help with a backlog, we would inspect commercial places also. Our studies of fire prevention and the laws were of great help to our group, and Captain Adams was pleased with our work as we progressed. I had divided the men into groups; everyone was satisfied with the arrangement, and all were compatible.

None questioned my being the leader, and the schedules were worked out to each one's satisfaction - it was a smooth operation - no favoritism - we were all firemen and all equal. Many times the men would congratulate me for the way I set things up, as they were content with the distribution of our work load. They wondered as to how I was selected as the leader, and none knew of the friendship between Captain Adams and myself; it all worked out fine. Our duties came to an end when we had our orders to report to headquarters to be promoted. Captain Adams thanked us all for a well done job - he was sorry to lose us, but soon would get another group to replace us. He was a fine gentleman, pleasant and well liked - all of us shook hands with him, as he congratulated each man on his promotion.

Our group arrived for promotion the next day excited with a feeling of well-being and exaltation, as we were about to be elevated to the rank of lieutenant. All our years of time spent "in the books" were coming to fruition. It was surely a feeling of exhilaration and reflection, looking back at the past years of studying and many times being deprived of social activities to keep on going for the "Brass Ring." It wasn't easy, and it was hard on the many students who did not make it. The initial promotion to lieutenant was always deemed to be the most difficult, as you had to get the first one before going any higher.

We were sworn in, given our lieutenant's insignias, and told that our assignment would appear on the

U.S. Army Photograph

Duties for Ed Schneider (in uniform, standing) included inspecting rooming houses for visitors to the 1938 World's Fair, and fire prevention demonstrations such as the one pictured above at Ft. Hamilton, NY.

Ed Schneider soon after his promotion to lieutenant in 1939.

night's orders - we had to wait to find out where we were being sent until that evening. I waited at a nearby firehouse for the messenger bringing the orders. I was assigned to Engine 29. I knew it was not in Brooklyn, but did not know where it was, as I was not familiar with units not in Brooklyn; I saw the low number and thought it was up in the Bronx someplace. I looked it up on the companies' directory - lower Manhattan - Chambers Street. That was easy traveling time for me - subway to City Hall station - I was happy that I didn't have to travel to the Bronx!

Many of my friends asked me who I knew to get such a good spot. I swear no one got it for me - that was the truth - the cards were dealt to me that way. It didn't take me long to find out what my friends meant; it sure was a place for inactivity. I was an "extra," and was sent to units to fill in for vacations. The units were downtown New York City, and the first month there I had one run! At Ladder 148 we would have 150 runs a month, and as aide to the chief we'd do 200 runs monthly. The next month I had one run - total in two months: two runs - no workers! The next month I had one run, so it was three months - three runs - no workers! I wasn't used to that, and wanted some action. We were working the 8 hour day then, and the system was being instituted by divisions, usually every three months. It was generally known that downtown was slow, but as you went north the work load got heavier into midtown, and the further north you went, the work load was the busiest in the city. Downtown used to get some very big fires, especially in the old loft buildings - fires that most always were fourth and fifth alarms. In the area of Wall Street on a weekend, everything was quiet - no activities going on and no office workers crowding the streets.

Sunday morning outdoor drills were held without any traffic interference - you had it all to yourself. I'd take the pumper and hose wagon around the block and lay two hose lines from the wagon for a deck-pipe stream, and the other a hand line. The chief would come around to supervise the drills, and compliment me when he saw both streams in operation. One such Sunday morning the chief asked me my name, was impressed by the drill, and asked me where I had worked before my promotion. When I told him I was aide to a chief, he said he was most happy to have me in his battalion. We became good friends as soon as he asked who I was aide to - he and Chief Lyons were good friends for years and he, as well as others, knew of his reputation.

One day I met a former fireman from Ladder 148, who was promoted to lieutenant before me, and was working in Brooklyn. I told him about downtown New York City, and he said he had an officer friend in the Assignment Bureau; he'd ask him to send me to a Brooklyn unit when the next division would get the three platoon system. The Assignment Bureau was charged with taking care of all of the administrative work, and they had one busy job in doing it. It was done by his friend - I was on the next assignment and transfer orders, and was sent to Brooklyn to the company where Chief Lyons was the captain, Ladder 122, back in Park Slope, next door to where I started out as a rookie.

Many changes had taken place over the past years, with new faces and a completely new staff of officers in both units. Again I had the good fortune of being with a wonderful well-liked captain, and a fine, decent and efficient chief! I was still an extra lieutenant, but my captain was designated an acting chief, and that kept me at my unit until he came back to us. Then I would go "carrying the bag," as extras had to do. That was fine with me - I got to work in practically all of our units and meet new men and officers. In time I was given the assignment from extra, to "relief," which was having three units, consisting of two consecutive tours of duty in each of the three, which made up my work week. From that I was eventually made a "steady" lieutenant in my own unit. There was much to do in training and drilling new men being appointed due to the increases of personnel for the three platoon system. After that a friend of mine retired from a nearby single engine company, and I was given the steady berth there. Working out of a single unit was most desirous, as there was always an officer coming in and going out at all change of tours.

I had the good fortune of having a captain whom I had been a fireman with at Ladder 148 - the one we nicknamed "Einstein" who had helped all of us youngsters with our studies. We shared many memories together, and he was as delighted to have me as his lieutenant as I was to have him as my captain. We had a good working efficient unit, were well regarded by our chiefs and other units that we responded with doing fire duty.

A former chief of department made a statement many years ago. He said: "A contented force is an efficient force." It does not imply that an officer should act as if he was in a popularity contest. The objective is to be fair but firm, and as a leader to learn to take orders before giving them, and show respect in order to get respect. It usually follows "Good officers make for a good company." We were all of that - our outfit had a very good reputation. We were in a heavy residential and commercial area, and our fire incidents ran in high figures each year. I couldn't have been happier, nor more content -

Engine 269 was a wonderful part of my life on the job - thanks to a great bunch of guys.

CHAPTER NINE

UP THE LADDER

Our skipper had been high up on the captain's list, and I too had passed the captain's exam with about a two-year wait. The years passed quickly enough, as we were one big happy group, and in due time I was promoted to captain and left 269, happy in knowing I had been sent to another well-regarded unit, but still feeling emotion for the great stay that I had had as a lieutenant there.

Examinations were not given too quickly in those years, and it developed that when the chief's test was held, my former skipper and myself took it; he formed our study group and we were "into the books" once again.

My tenure as a lieutenant (except the New York City part) was in the 10th division, which was under the command of Deputy Chief Kidney, the division commander. I had many fires when I was aide to Chief Lyons, operating under his command. He was an extremely efficient man, a very quiet person who gave the appearance of having "ice water" in him at all times; he was always cool and calm - never boisterous - whether at fires or at his desk in quarters. As an aide I had a close relationship with him. He was so quiet, that it was generally said one couldn't get closer than an arm's length to him. He truly served as a model worthy of imitation to subordinates - an exemplary person. I believe it was an observance of me as his aide that he gave me many assignments of trust, plus favorable

Chief Thomas J. Lyons, left, at his retirement dinner in 1958. Chief Schneider is shown presenting to his mentor and idol a book, "This is Your Nite."

consideration. For instance, there was the time a vacant July vacation suddenly and unexpectedly opened up. Vacations were drawn - not selected - and I had drawn December. I got a phone call from Chief Kidney himself, asking if I would like to have a July vacation which would begin in two days. "Asking" me? There were thirty-two units in the division with lieutenants, and he "asked" me! I excitedly accepted it and began thanking him when he said: "No more thanks, lieutenant, you deserve it!" End of conversation!

74

During the absence of a captain in a unit, who is the company commander, it is usually the senior lieutenant who assumes those duties. There was a unit in the division that was without its captain, and also its lieutenants. Chief Kidney called me, telling me he was designating me to that unit as company commander! Again, he had all the lieutenants in his division to select from, and he chose me, a "Johnny come lately" - and I wasn't on the captain's list either. I was pleased that he gave me the recognition to perform an assignment of higher authority. I guess all I can say is that he liked what he saw in me.

It was a warm sunny day in August and I had just completed my roll call entries in the company journal for my 4 to 12 hour tour. I looked over the previous tours entries, signed my name and rank, and as I closed the book I sat there at the watch desk thinking of what kind of a tour it would be - busy or quiet. I began to think of a good friend of mine - a policeman in Jersey, and recalled how he would most always catch a heavy workload as he started his tour. Why was I thinking like that! Was it an omen? I stopped those thoughts and joined the men standing in front of quarters. The entrance doors of the firehouse were open - the cook was getting the meal list together - everything was just perfectly normal at the time. Then it all began - by a woman who stopped in front of quarters.

An extremely refined, well dressed woman approached us, and speaking to none of us in particular, asked: "Who is the commanding officer?" I heard her and immediately said to myself, "Oh-Oh- who would ask for the commanding officer?" That was strictly a military term. The fireman nearest to her pointed to me and said:

"The Lieutenant is in charge."

She walked towards me, and I had strong suspicion that she was under the influence of alcohol. She directed her remarks to me, by stating, "Lieutenant, I want you to make an arrest of a woman who is in a bar nearby which I just left. She is drinking and neglected her baby who is in a carriage crying, outside of the bar."

Getting a full handle on the situation, I answered her politely and courteously that this was not within my authority - we are firemen, not policemen. I suggested to her to look for a police car and tell them her story. She was adamant and insisted upon taking "proper action!"

This woman was a high class person, well bred and well spoken. She held my interest in the fine way she was dressed. Her speech and manners indicated beyond doubt that she was cultured and probably an important person of sorts. The fact was, she was under the influence - she was in a bar drinking, and it showed.

People were now stopping to listen and rubberneck. She walked to the watch desk and demanded the housewatchman to get up from his chair and give her his seat. I told him to stay in his seat; there was no way she was going to take over the desk. She told me that I was no gentleman and then walked to the front of the engine and sat on the extended bumper, saying she would not leave until I took "proper action" on her complaint about the mother drinking in the bar and her baby crying outside.

The rubberneckers grew into a large crowd of watchers. I used all of my persuasiveness and reasoning to get her to leave, but she wouldn't get off the engine bumper. I told her that if we had to respond to an alarm she was going to be physically removed, as she was interfering with our operations. She demanded to use the phone at the watch desk, which of course I refused. This was now getting out of control. I had the men looking for a police patrol car, but none were passing.

All this time I was polite and firm, but getting nowhere with her. Finally I said to her, "Madam, I'm going to call the police and have you arrested for interfering with our duties." She didn't bat an eye, replying, "Go ahead!" Again, I tried to tell her this would be embarrassing to her and her family by having her arrested and going to court. She would also probably be charged with disorderly conduct and be shamed by it all. There was only one way. She would have to be removed, either by us if we got a run, or by the police.

This was the era when people would scream "Don't you touch me. Take your hands off me - I'll sue you, etc." The die was cast - I called the dispatcher to have a police car come to quarters. As the police car pulled up, the patrolman was given the cause by his dispatcher, and as he got through the crowd to me I filled him in - get her out of here! He went to her - told her to leave - and she refused. Within seconds he grabbed her and carried her out of the quarters past the crowd, tossed her into the back of the police car and took her away as the crowd cheered.

I had the entrance doors closed and breathed relief as I rethought the events and made an entry of the unusual occurrence in the journal.

This was truly a case of "a nothing" escalating into an undreamed of situation. Not long afterwards I was called to the phone. It was the police desk lieutenant saying I would have to go to the police station and sign the complaint against the woman. I told him: "No way, Lieutenant. You know I can't be forced to leave my quarters - it is now a police matter. Have the officer sign the complaint - he saw what happened - I'll be the witness, but I'm not going to the station house!" We agreed on that and hung up.

Ten minutes later, the police lieutenant called me again. He said, "Lieutenant, there's something that the woman just said - she's willing to drop everything if the policeman will apologize and won't arrest her. Will you go along with that?" "Of course," I said, "but what about the policeman - will he apologize for doing his job?" The Lieutenant said the policeman didn't want to, so I asked to speak to him. This officer was no stranger to me - I knew him well. He agreed. That's when he told me the lady was the wife of a well-known army general, and had second thoughts about what she did. The policeman, the woman, the police lieutenant and myself all said "amen - case closed!"

Attaining the rank of captain is a giant step forward; a lieutenant's duties were few - the captain had many. The captain is the commander of a unit and is totally responsible and accountable for the discipline and efficiency of his unit. That, in brief, is the "whole ball of wax." The manner in which a company is managed - diligently or without interest, reflects credit or discredit upon its leadership. It doesn't take too long for superiors to notice how a company is performing; that's how reputations are made - one way or the other.

A recognized principle of truth is that some persons approaching retirement have a tendency to slow down and show less effort. The interest, or feeling of attention to matters begins to dwindle and diminish - the enthusiasm and zeal is less - hence the saying: "A new broom sweeps clean." This feeling can be noted in the business world, occupational or professional field. It was the same on our job for those who had their retirement papers in. I saw it happen when I took command of Engine 226, but did not have any ill feelings about it; there were many things that needed to be corrected and I went to work on them willingly.

I had been detailed there for several months while attending officer's school as a lieutenant, and the skipper and I became very good friends. He ran a good company and was well thought of by superiors and the men. When my assignment there was over and I went back to my own unit, he told me he was sorry I had to leave, and how satisfied he had been having me there. He was a real nice guy and we had a close relationship. I told him it was my pleasure to serve under him; I considered him a good friend. When the time came for his retirement some years later, he phoned me to let me know he was retiring. He knew I would be promoted to captain shortly, and maybe I could get his spot. I was the only one he "tipped off" to the vacancy with the "inside" information - he hoped I could get it. I thanked him for being so thoughtful and wished him the best in retirement. He retired - I got the company.

The members of the company and I were no strangers to each other, and they were pleased to see me come back as captain. Our study subjects over the years had included personnel management, plus I had taken a separate course in supervision; it all was useful. I realized I had to go slowly, get organized, and set up my priorities. There would not be any hurried or drastic changes made - or too many - that would only lead to confusion. I found out there was much to be done administratively. It was a challenge which I willingly accepted.

Ed Schneider is beaming after his promotion to Captain and assignment to Engine Co. 226 in 1944. Note the poster of The Midnight Alarm *adorning the wall.*

Each captain has to account for all equipment, tools, hose, appliances, etc. This is done yearly by submitting his booklet of yearly property returns. That's where I started, by taking inventory from cellar to roof, and comparing the previous return of the former captain with what was actually on hand. I gave each man an assignment to take a count of everything - it turned out to be difficult and time consuming before the job was finished.

Record keeping left much to be desired in many units. There were many deliveries of supplies and equipment received and sent out over the period of a year, and records were many times inadequate and incomplete. When hose, equipment, etc., was sent out, it was necessary to be receipted for. If your property was not returned by the end of the year, the receipt had to be sent with the property return to account for it. I found that on paper I was carrying more than what I had on hand - that became a problem.

Supplies, such as brooms, mops, pails, stationery, etc., were expendable, so that was simple to take care of. The big items, such as hose and tools, etc., had to balance out - either you had them on hand, or had receipts for them. Many times coal was carried as plentiful on hand, but the coal bins were nearly empty - and so it went, on and on with the inventory.

I surely didn't want to contradict the figures of the past. For instance, I was short 19 lengths of hose - unaccounted for - plus other items. I went to the "Boss" for his advice. I did not want to implicate the former skipper on any shortages. I defined the problem, and a solution was worked out to everyone's satisfaction. Within three days I had 19 new lengths of hose delivered to my quarters, plus other unaccounted for items - case closed!

Tricks being played was always going on by the jokesters. One day, the most despicable "joke" was put over on this poor lieutenant - and believe me there wasn't anyone laughing as soon as it happened and I heard of it.

The lieutenant's office was on the second floor, with his desk close to a window facing the back yard. The lieutenant was at his desk, and all was serene and quiet. The firehouse clown had put together a dummy with catsup on his face and went to the roof. From a position on the roof, directly in line with the lieutenant's window, he tossed the dummy off the roof! The poor lieutenant almost had a heart attack as the dummy whizzed past his view! The clown can running down and shouted a fireman just fell off the roof! My office was on the top floor, and as I heard the dope shouting, I jumped up and grabbed him as he was running downstairs, demanding to know what happened. He laughingly told me of his "joke!" I ran down to the lieutenant's office and found the poor fellow hysterical with fright at what he had seen. I immediately told him it wasn't so, and used all my persuasiveness to make him understand what really had happened. I calmed him down, and he understood - but he was still nervous and shaken. I went after the clown as I never went after anyone. I chastised and criticized him severely. There wasn't any middle ground here - I was furious!

I told the lieutenant I would handle this dope, and I would hand out the punishment. I had him apologize to the lieutenant for his stupidity and had him report to my office immediately. I let him know he had a twisted mind pulling off such a stunt, and gave him extra work assignments for every tour he and I worked. I would decide when to end the punishment period. I ordered him to report to me personally each tour for the extra work and I worked his butt off.

At a much later date, the captain preferred charges against him for intoxication. He drew a ten-day fine and was transferred to Harlem, where he got plenty of fire duty. (This was his second offense for intoxication.) When he went to Harlem, the first time he did the same thing there, that captain gave him a same charge, which resulted in his dismissal from the department.

The shouting officer is the worst and truly is a sign of weakness plus incompetence. We had a fire in the backyard of a florist shop - burning wreaths - flames were visible upon arrival. The chief saw the flames and yelled out loud, "Someone send a second alarm! Send a second alarm!" The fire was extinguished with one hose stream!

Another time with the same chief, we went to a store and dwelling fire. There wasn't any visible fire or smoke. The store was closed. We were directed there by the person who sent the alarm. The chief had not arrived with us. I felt the glass of the door and showcases, and it was so hot and smoke stained I realized there was a very hot fire in there. I immediately ordered a hose line stretched to the door. The ladder company was with us, and I ordered a twenty-foot portable ladder to the entrance and gave orders to use the ladder to break the door in as soon as we got our water.

"Mr. Shouter" arrived and screamed at me, "Break open the door - break the glass!" I said to him, "We will, as soon as our water comes - it's on the way - feel the glass - it's red hot!" He continued to shout as our water came. The ladder was set into the door and broken open, water went on the fire at the same instant - a back draft was avoided and the fire extinguished. Of course the chief knew the potential, but was very excited - once again!

It was my day off and I went to a store for some needed medication for my wife. As I was returning home - only one block away - I heard apparatus responding, and when they stopped there was a fire raging through the top floor and roof of a frame dwelling. The dense, acrid smoke and stifling heat which had filled the building had banked up in the attic and on the top flight of stairs. I ran to the scene as units were arriving - some of the units were from my area of command.

I assumed command and ordered hose lines stretched and ladders raised. it was an extremely smokey fire - resulting from a delayed discovery and delayed alarm. My co-worker, Acting Battalion Chief Sullivan arrived and I reported what I had done and then entered the burning building to direct and assist in advancing the hose line up an unusually narrow stairway which was filled with gases, intense heat and thick smoke. When we reached the top floor I ordered the men to cover me with their hose stream, while I searched the floor. In one room I found a man unconscious on the floor under bedding and chairs. I removed the obstacles and started to drag and carry him out to safety. I was now close to exhaustion and called for assistance; a fireman came to my aid, and we carried the unconscious man to the head of the stairway. The fireman then took him to the street.

The Division Chief had responded to the fire and assumed command. I apprised him of conditions and progress. I did not have any firefighting clothing on - not even boots - and I informed him I was on my day off and had pitched in. He saw I was wringing wet from the hose lines; he took the needed information, complimented me for my action and dismissed me, telling me to go home and get out of my wet clothes. He wrote a meritorous duty report on my actions, recommending a class one award for me, for which upon later approval I was given the Brooklyn Citizens Medal and the Department Medal of Valor.

Annually the department presents medals to men, who during the year performed conspicuous acts of bravery, and to the next of kin of those who sacrificed their lives in the performance of duty. When a superior believes such an act of bravery was performed, he writes a meritorious duty report of the member's action. He then makes his judgment as to the degree of the act. Degrees are: Class 1 - Extreme Personal Risk, Class 2 - Great Personal Risk, Class 3 - Unusual Personal Risk.

All reports are submitted to headquarters and reviewed by the Board of Merit. They either approve or disapprove. Those approved are awarded a medal, donated yearly by citizens, department societies and associations. In addition, the department itself also awards their own department medal.

I was awarded the Brooklyn Citizens Medal and Department Medal for my act. It was endowed by a committee of Brooklynites (1896) viz: "To be given to the most deserving firemen in Brooklyn, and shall be selected by the fire department of the city of New York."

The ceremonies are usually held at City Hall Plaza - presentations are given by the mayor, with full attendance of the fire commissioner and chief of department and staff chiefs.

My wife and children were there for the big occa-

The Honorable William O'Dwyer
Mayor of the City of New York
and
Frank J. Quayle
Fire Commissioner
request the honor of your presence at the

Presentation of Medals

*to Members of the Fire Department for distinguished service and to the next of
kin of those who sacrificed their lives in the performance of duty during 1949*

Monday, June nineteenth, Nineteen hundred fifty
at 12.30 p. m., The Plaza, City Hall

Brooklyn Citizens Medal

AND DEPARTMENT MEDAL

Awarded to

Captain Edwin F. Schneider
ENGINE CO. 226
(Now Chief—48th Battalion)

For assisting in the rescue of a man from a fire at 7801 4th Ave., Brooklyn, on October 16, 1949.

THIS rescue was in a 3-story, frame dwelling occupied as a rooming-house. Captain Schneider was off duty and strolling in the neighborhood. When he heard the apparatus responding he ran to the scene. The fire was raging through the entire top floor and roof. The dense, acrid smoke and stifling heat which filled the building had banked up in the attic and on the top flight of stairs. Captain Schneider assumed command and ordered the firemen to raise ladders and stretch hose lines. When Acting Battalion Chief Francis E. Sullivan arrived, Schneider reported what he had done and then entered the burning building to assist the members of Engine Co. 241 advance the hose line to the top floor. Schneider and the members of Engine Co. 241 sustained severe punishment in taking the hose line up an unusually narrow stairway which was filled with gases, intense heat and thick smoke. Upon reaching the top floor, Schneider ordered the firemen to cover him with the hose stream while he searched the floor. In one room he found Mr. Anthony Constantino unconscious on the floor under bedding and chairs. Schneider removed the chairs and bedding and started to drag Mr. Constantino to safety. Schneider was now close to a state of exhaustion and called for assistance. Fireman John I. Butterly, H. & L. Co. 149, rushed to his aid and helped Captain Schneider carry the unconscious man to the head of the stairway. Fireman Butterly then took Mr. Constantino to the street.

sion, watching the mayor pin my medal onto my uniform coat. They were so proud of me as I was of them - it was also my daughter's birthday.

Like many other captains, I was away from my company as acting battalion chief for lengthy periods for vacancies, vacations, etc. New men were appointed to my company that I never met. I believe I spent more time away as acting chief than as captain in my own unit, especially when the promotion list for chief was released and I was on it!

Captain Schneider's chief's car during the winter of 1948 when he was acting chief of the 48th Battalion.

Capt. (Acting Batt. Chief) Schneider is on the right in the front row at an Engine Co. 240 inspection in May 1949. It was at this station that he buffed as a teenager. Eighth from the left in the white cap is Capt. Frank Carney, who was Chief Schneider's lieutenant at Ladder 148. Capt. Carney also was promoted to Battalion Chief.

CHAPTER TEN

I'M A
FIRE CHIEF!

There were many vacancies for chiefs, but promotions were slow in coming. About 25 of us on the chief's list were acting out of title as acting battalion chief. We held a meeting of eligibles and formed "The Chief Eligible Association." I was selected as its president of a triumvirate - three of us sharing the authority in case one of us should be absent. We had many meetings with the fire commissioner and headquarter chiefs. The chiefs were sympathetic to our group and all for us. Our problem was with the budget bureau and the politicians, and there were many disappointments, delays and promises.

Chief Lyons used to say: "If you keep throwing mud up against a wall, some of it is bound to stick!" We put in a great deal of time, effort and energy into making our voices heard. I had made many friends and acquaintances, politically and socially, as well as the high levels of headquarter chiefs. I attended and spoke before the mayor and Board of Estimate at budget hearings in making a case for the filling of vacancies.

At our eligible meetings, progress reports of our activities were made, and ideas discussed. We weren't getting any place and all of us were aware of it; many times tempers were short - most of us were acting chiefs and wanted the promotion - we were doing the work, the vacancies were there, and many men wanted to organize a movement to get us back to our units instead of

Promotion day to chief, April 1, 1950

working out of title. All of us shared the same frustrations: I volunteered to step down as president of the group, and have someone else take over. Before the meeting ended, I was given a vote of confidence and remained as president.

I had an idea - one picture is worth 1,000 words - I had each eligible survey his division for vacancies and send me the results. When completed, I bought a large piece of cardboard - 15" x 15" - and boxed it, numbering the battalions in numerical order. I then red-crayoned each box where there were vacancies. Each box was 3" x 3" in size and the whole project had so many red boxes, they easily outnumbered the whites.

Our perseverance paid off - the red boxes did it - the right people were contacted and were impressed. I had a life long real good friend who was in a high ranking position of city government. His credentials were impeccable; he was known for his moral principles and standards; in a word, he could knock on any door and it would be opened for him. I showed him the board and explained our problem - it turned out favorably for us. It wasn't long after that we were all promoted.

When I was promoted I remained in the same assignment I had as acting battalion chief. The difference now being I would get chief's pay - work was the same - there wasn't any extra compensation for acting out of title. I still was a relief, doing two tours in two battalions. I turned in my captain's silver insignias for the gold insignias chief's rank.

The prophecy of my buff days came true twice for me - one being an officer, the other becoming a chief. What a terrific feeling of accomplishment after all of the years of studying and self denial in getting there, seeing those predictions come true.

I sincerely regret that the two men who made them didn't live to see it happen - From buff to chief!

There was a fireman in my quarters who had a drinking problem. Yet he was well liked, always did a good days work and was known as a good fireman. He was single and lived with his aged mother, being her means of support. Time after time he'd come to work under the influence in bad shape. He could not do his assigned duties such as housewatch, committee work (cleaning quarters), etc. His duties would have to be picked up by other men, and were resented.

One day I heard loud voices of the men cleaning the dormitory - they were angry because they were doing someone elses' duties, and were saying so. I went to them and asked some questions and got some not-too-favorable answers in return. Their complaint was having to do someone's work who was "sick," and this was an ongoing occurrence.

I had observed this situation, and knew something had to be done to correct it. I went to the captain of his unit and put it squarely up to him by asking him what, if anything, was being done about this. He replied "nothing!" Now that in itself was seemingly O.K. by not taking disciplinary action. However some kind of help was needed for the drinking man, as he had been disciplined in the previous units he had been in. I told the captain the situation wasn't getting any better, and I stepped into the picture.

It is known that the men working in quarters where the chief puts up are in daily touch with the chief, and likewise, the chief with his men. There is a commonly existing closeness between them, as they live, eat, and work together. At times there might even be a little bit of favoritism because of this closeness of being together. The men get to know their chief, and the chief gets a better perspective of his men. I was no exception to this; we had a comfortable feeling and relationship. The closeness bred camaraderie.

The first move I made was to call into my office two of the brothers for their help. I asked them to get the fellow straightened out with coffee and a shower and when he was in good shape to bring him to my office. This request was not enthusiastically accepted, but I reminded them of past favors which were done on their behalf. I let them know I was going to try to help this addicted drinker, as we agreed he needed help. They went to work on him.

I got the man's personnel file from his captain and found out he had two ten days pay fines against him in units he had served in before he came to us. All this in a short period of time - for each offense he was transferred. This was serious - two strikes! One more and he would surely receive the ultimate: dismissal from the job!

The two guys did a good job. They gave him coffee, a shower and shave, and something to eat. They told him I wanted to see him, and they brought him to me. Tom was looking good, and I thanked the two brothers for their good work; I said to Tom, "Sit down here at my desk - we're going to have a talk."

He was receptive to my invitation to talk it out. I "shadow-boxed" with him for a few minutes, talking about the job, his good qualities, etc. and then got into the matter at hand.

I remember very vividly saying I was a fire chief - not a priest - and that drew an immediate kindly and appreciative smile from him. Then I told him, no matter what, that he was drinking because he had a problem - that drinking is an escape from reality - and I put it squarely up to him by asking him what his problem was!

There was sadness in his face and tears in his eyes, as he started to talk. He seemed more and more ashamed with guilt of his behavior, and then the tears started to really flow. He asked me: "Chief, will you please close the door?" When I closed my office door, he cried softly, and said to me, "Yes Chief, I have a problem."

I had learned from courses I had taken and from experiences with others that the first thing to do is *listen*, as many times a troubled person in reality only thinks he has a problem. The listener has to put it all together and decide for himself if there really is a problem. It so happens that there may not be a problem, and this is readily discernable to the listener; this could relate to working conditions, "being picked on," or a personal affair.

He was crying all the more as he began to open up, and I felt heartedly sorry for him. There he sat, a good person, sobbing out his story. I listened very attentively at his every word. He told me he was keeping company with a woman and they were to be married. When Tom told her they'd have to live with his old 85-year-old mother as he was her only son and means of support, she became furious at him. "No way," she said and immediately called off the marriage! He continued, "Chief, that in itself was hard to take, but, within two weeks, she got married to someone else!"

That was it! I needed to hear no more - there wasn't

any problem to solve - I had all the facts necessary, as I began to explain to him how fortunate he was not to have married her! I told him all she wanted was a "meal ticket" out of him! She wanted the security of a "pay day," and then a pension when he died! Couldn't he see that? She was not in love with him! I kept telling him! - "Getting some other guy to marry her was enough proof of that, can't you understand?"

Then as my remarks took hold of him, I'll never forget the change of expression which came over him. He put both hands to his face and said, "Chief - I never realized that!" He repeated that over and over, and finally admitted to me that he "saw the light!"

What he termed a problem, was indeed a self-thought problem. But the reality of it all was "No problem!"

We sat talking about all that was said, and he thanked me for the help I gave him. I told him now it was up to him to "shape up," and he promised he would. I told him I'd help him; he kept his promise.

The first thing I did to see him through his ordeal, was to arrange a medical leave for him. This was accomplished by deviating from the staight and direct course, with the help of friends in higher places whom I called upon. They were the ones who really helped - among whom were my dear friends of many years - one being our chaplain, who had personally known about "The Problem," as it was called. Another good and close friend who directly aided by his understanding, was a boro commander, who, upon receipt of the medical leave report, phoned me. He personally knew of Tom's two ten days pay fines, and gave me his support when I apprised him of the particulars. The whole endeavor was one of team effort, each having a part in Tom's rehabilitation.

Tom was eventually placed on light duty, and I assigned him to messenger duty. He was fine and completely recovered, although he was frail and pale looking. He remained on light duty for quite a period of time. There were many retirement parties which he attended; he'd have his soda, and always got a big hand from the brothers "who knew him when." He finally retired on pension, and from day one of his recovery, to the day he died - ten years later - never had he taken any kind of an alcoholic drink - he had kept his promise! He married a widow with young children, and when I went to his wake, I heard stories told to me about his being a great husband and a devoted father to the children - he was truly loved by them all. He had acknowledged the third tradition of the A.A., viz: "A desire to stop drinking." He won the fight, and I'll always remember him for it. May he rest in peace!

I've previously written about "fate and destiny," but there is an instance in my tenure as chief which could have ended in tragedy were it not for fate taking over. The newspapers could have headlined it: "SIX FIRE FIGHTERS BURNED TO DEATH".

Upon my arrival to a box alarm about 2 a.m., I was confronted with a very serious fire in a bar and grill on the first floor, and two stories over same.

Fire and smoke conditions were extremely heavy - there was a delayed discovery of the fire which resulted in a delayed alarm. The premises were closed and my first concern was the possible life hazard on the top floor and the lateral possible extension of fire at the top, via the cockloft to the adjoining buildings, all of which were the same height. Hose lines were placed into the front and rear. Alongside the bar entrance was an enclosed stairway leading to the second floor, and a hose line was stretched up the stairway. I had the ladder companies raise ladders and search and ventilate, and ascertain if fire had extended into the cockloft. I ordered a second alarm transmitted.

The engine company positioned on the stairs had advanced their line to the top of the stairway landing, and had a good working heavy stream sweeping the second floor from the landing. I gave my orders to my aide for incoming units, and then went up the stairway to observe conditions. The officer and his men were crouched on the landing and doing a good job with their stream and holding their position, making a stand and trying to advance in on the fire with extreme heavy smoke.

When I had joined them in their operations, I immediately noted the absence of flame and could not observe fire. The smoke condition was so bad we could not advance the line and then I noted the smoke was changing into a thick black, brownish color and was twisting and starting to roll over our heads. I recognized a "backdraft" in the making, and immediately ordered everyone to "back out" and abandon the hose line. The officer at my side said, "It's O.K. chief, we can make it!" I repeated, "Back out, get out," in no uncertain loud voice which had its affect and we all scooted down the stairs.

We retreated and had just reached the sidewalk - only ten to fifteen feet from the base of the stairs and were pulling the hose line down backwards, when the backdraft happened. The stairway which we were on only seconds before was a sea of fire, and fire was leaping out of the broken windows of the second floor.

My additional units arrived and were placed in operations. The cockloft exposure was negative and we confined and extinguished the fire. We later found the body of the dishwasher on the floor area - nothing could have saved him.

The officer and men whom I ordered to "back out" stood on the sidewalk and saw the stairs on fire, and the whole second floor in flames. They quickly sensed what would have happened to them and to me, had I not ordered them out.

I had great admiration for that officer and his men for their dedication. Their attempt to hold their position under extremely serious conditions was understandable. They shook their heads in disbelief as they attacked the flames from the retreated position.

Later on, one of the men got me alone and said, "Chief, you're a genius!" I responded by telling him, "No way! Any chief could have done the same! I was in the right place at the right time." I continued, "I was caught in a backdraft many years ago, was burned on my face and hands and was hospitalized. It was that and all my years of experience and study, plus the hand of fate and of course the Almighty. Genius? Hell no! Fate - you bet!"

CHAPTER ELEVEN

"I'LL HOOK YOU UP!"

I had one of the the most unusual experiences of my career one day while I was acting deputy chief in our division. The dispatcher phoned me, advising me of a man on the outside ledge of the 14th floor of the Veterans Administration Hospital, threatening to jump. The deputy chief is always apprised and notified of all unusual occurrences. I responded to the scene.

It is known that "copy cats" will imitate past events, and this was one of those cases. It perhaps was the case of a "jumper" outside a hotel window in New York City that triggered many of these particular incidents. It was given much publicity over the air, and in the papers; pictures showed him on the ledge with the police and clergy trying to talk him out of it, to no avail - he jumped to his death. Our study group discussed this, and sought ways to approach it, if ever we were called for help in such a situation. As I was responding, these thoughts went through my mind, and I prepared my plan mentally prior to my arrival.

The crowds on the V.A. grounds were enormous. Cars had stopped and parked on the grass, and the reported news on the radio brought hundreds upon hundreds of onlookers and curiosity seekers; as a matter of fact, there were some trying to make bets on whether the fellow would or would not jump! That was revolting to me - here was a potential suicide, and the crowds were shouting "Jump - jump," and "Don't jump - don't jump!"

The police were there in large numbers with their emergency vans, as they were called when it all started. I inquired as to who was in charge, and was brought to the commanding officer, Captain Maguire, whom I shall always remember as one fine person. I saluted him, identified myself and instantly asked him if I could render any assistance, knowing and telling him that he was in charge. He thanked me and asked me to stay. We then had a conference of events - I was very impressed by his leadership - as we discussed "ways and means" of getting the fellow in. I have always admired the police and had many friends in their department. It's difficult to understand the in-fighting between the two departments today - we always got along great with each other at emergencies and were always cooperative.

I had told Captain Maguire of a plan we had developed while studying in anticipation of such an event, after the New York City case mentioned at a hotel. He remembered it well as I explained it to him. I again reminded him that it was his operation - he was in total command, and I would not usurp his authority. He said that never crossed his mind - that we would work together in a 100% combined effort and cooperation to achieve the objective of preventing a loss of life. We respected each other's rank, as well as person and were amiable with and agreeable to each other throughout the entire operation.

I instructed my aide to notify the dispatcher of particulars and have an engine and ladder company and chief respond to the scene. I well remembered the lessons taught us as youngsters by our lieutenants - "When you are promoted, always do something about something!" This was a classical case of "doing something!"

When the apparatus arrived, I gave instructions to get two large (10') hooks (used for pulling ceilings), ropes and the life net. We could go to the floor below (13th), secure the poles by rope to each side of the atlas net, and when all was in readiness our men would put it out of the window and hold it there. We would now have a safety net right below the would-be-jumper, and catch him in it. Captain Maguire was impressed - he obtained a rope cargo net from his van, and that was brought to the 15th floor (one above). That was the plan - over and below the jumper to snare him.

I had my aide call the dispatcher to notify a nearby church to send spiritual aide - we did not know the man's faith. We also had the doctors give us needed information about his family and notify someone to respond. We later found out the man was Jewish, and I had a nearby synagogue called, which sent a rabbi. We found out the man was single, and his mother, sister and brother came at the hospital's request. The hospital psychiatrists were also talking to the man - he was still out there and had been, for many hours without any results.

We were now ready with our equipment - all set up at the 13th floor. Captain Maguire had his cargo net on the 15th floor. The subject was still sitting on the 14th floor ledge. At command, the cargo net was thrown out to snare and get him - we had our net out to catch him - it all sounded feasible and capable of accomplishment. The ledge was 4' to 5' wide, and when he heard the voices he looked up and saw the cargo net coming at him - he leaped away like a rabbit on his haunches as the net nearly had him. From our position we saw what happened and pulled in our safety net - it was impossible to get him, as he could easily leap away from us.

The doctors in charge were furious at our attempted "snare and catch" operation. They vehemently expressed their criticism of our actions and said they would hold us directly responsible if we did anything further and caused his death.

Captain Maguire and I held a conference in a private room. We both agreed to halt operations, as it was easy for the subject to leap and run across the ledge, and defeat our every move. The envisioned newspaper headlines saying "FIREMEN CAUSE DEATH" was too risky. We put aside one remaining plan I had ready for getting him. We agreed it was well worth using, and would work. However, the obstacle was the wide ledge he was on; he had moved his position many times all day, and when he'd see the new attempt made, and being able not to escape, we felt that would make him jump - if he was going to!

My plan was this: we would have two firemen outflank him - one on his left, and one on his right; the men would have the bowline knots on, which we used for getting people out from up above. The bowline and bight was made up of loops around each leg to the groin, and then looped around the chest. Then with the long end being played out, the men would move towards him safely on the ledge. It was an evolution used many times successfully at rescues. The subject would be grabbed on the ledge by both firemen, as they closed in on him simultaneously. However, as stated, it was a high risk operation - when he realizes he couldn't escape in either direction - would he jump?

The crowds were getting larger as time went on. I had the ropes taken off my men, and we stood by awaiting developments. I dismissed the units I had waiting - no need for them. The rabbi and mother, sister and brother arrived and talked to the subject. All he did was shout and curse at them and wouldn't come in. We were back to square one!

I had my aide notify the boro commander of conditions, and he in turn notified the chief of department - this was the chain of command for unusual conditions. The boro commander responded, and I apprised him of our actions. He approved of the rope evolution attempt I had - I let him know what the doctors told us, and whatever happened now would be his responsibility as chief in command. He then told me to try and get him by myself, with the bowline and bight rope tied onto me. I thought it over and said I'd do it, with reservations.

I was tied with the loops on my legs - no rope around my chest. I knew as soon as he saw the rope, it would endanger the chance. My men held the rope taut, as I advanced to the open window where he was, taking steps inch by inch. He saw me coming and shouted at me "Get away - you cop!" I stopped and told him I was not a cop, but a fireman. His face lit up and he said, "Fireman? I love firemen!" I then started inching towards him, and he asked if any gambling was done in the firehouse, and if so, was I a gambler. I told him, "Sure I'm a gambler - why?" I was getting closer to him all the time. He said, "Let's take a gamble - you and I! O.K.?" I said, "What's the bet?" "You come and get me and the mayor will give you a medal," he replied. "Oh yea," I said - "What's the rest of the bet?" I was almost at him - one foot away. He said, "If you don't get me - you and I fall 14 floors to our deaths!" That was it! I told him that's a hell of a bad bet and made a grab for him. I actually got to touch him as he sprang away from his position cursing and shouting at me. That was the end of that episode, but far from the end of what was ahead - it would be a long day and night.

To be perfectly direct and frank, the arrival of the boro commander was upsetting to me. His reputation was widely known throughout the job as a shouter and loud mouth. He completely lacked delicacy and refinement of performance. He was crude and uncouth. This is said without any uneasiness or hesitation. Our paths frequently crossed at fires or incidents, or at quarters. He had a bad track record with subordinates - he was not liked as a man or a chief. As soon as I saw him arrive at the scene, I sensed trouble. As an example of his rudeness, this is how he greeted me on his arrival: "Hey Schneider - wadda ya got?"

Our other boro chiefs were men of class and quality, with excellent credentials and reputations. They gave and received the respect of everyone, and were well liked. I would have been elated to have one of them respond and receive their advice - I knew them personally - they were truly gentlemen and my good friends. However, it wasn't my good fortune. The one who everyone had no use for responded. My gut feeling was he wouldn't add one iota of assistance to us, but only cause confusion to our efforts, which were now at a standstill.

My arrival time was 2 P.M. - it was now 6 P.M. - change of tour time. I sent my aide back to quarters with the car for my relief to come (a standard routine). When he arrived, I brought him up to date and reported to the boro chief that I was relieved and leaving. That's when my trouble and the fireworks began!

Upon hearing that, he screamed at me, saying: "You're staying here - you're not going anywhere!" Rank or no rank, I went back at him telling him my tour was over and I was properly relieved. Within seconds there was a heavy confrontation - I couldn't believe what was happening! It went from an argument to push - from push to shove - and from shove to battle! I did not back down from my position and told him he couldn't order me to stay. I'm sure the fact that I went eyeball to eyeball with him in my determination really sent him out of control. His authority and order being challenged was more than he could stomach. He had to know he was wrong - my relief was in - I wasn't needed there. His anger turned to a rage as he screamed at me, "I'll hook you up! I'll hook you up!"

"Hook you up" was the vernacular used in the job for preferring charges against a member. I said to him, "Go ahead - hook me up and make a damn fool out of yourself altogether." I insisted that I wanted him to give me charges. But in my heart I knew he was a barking dog with no bite. I told him I never had a charge on my record, but I'd welcome his!

What could it be? Insubordination? Disobedience of his order which was by whim and impulsiveness? He was not only out of control with anger at me, he was being ridiculous!

My relief stood there in disbelief. This was my fight - not his - and rightly so he didn't take part in it. Mr. Repulsive ordered him back to the division, turned away from me and left the scene! I was caught between the proverbial rock and a hard place!

I had dismissed the units I had called, but gave orders for two men to stay and leave the ropes. Captain Maguire couldn't believe what happened. We went to an empty room, had sandwiches and coffee, and we just sat and talked.

An hour later the Chief of Department showed up to see what was going on. I informed him of our efforts and what the doctors had told us. I also told him of the confrontation with the Boro Chief, hoping that he'd see it my way and bring back my relief. He never said one word - he only looked at the subject on the ledge and left!

There he was - in a sitting position on that ledge - no one even bothered to talk to him; it was "wait and see" from here on in, and getting later and later into the night. Around 2 A.M. the hospital doctors came to Captain Maguire and myself and said, "Take him in - we give up on him!" They revoked our responsibility and assumed it themselves. I advised the dispatcher to notify the Chief of Department and call me back. He called me back and said the Chief of Department would respond - don't do anything until he arrived.

A short time later the Chief of Department arrived with two firemen from a rescue unit and ropes. I had previously told him about my rope try, and immediately sensed what he was going to do - I was right! We saw each rescue man get roped up with the bowline of loops on each leg. What I didn't understand was, how come my men weren't being used - why the two rescue men? I never said a word - just watched. One fireman went out the window onto the ledge on the left side, some 20 feet away from the subject. The other fireman did the same from the right side, and my men held and played out the rope holding them secure.

The moment of truth had come. Each rescue man started walking down the ledge towards the subject and the closer they got to him, the more he screamed at them saying he would jump! The men paid no attention to his screaming and closed the gap - he never made an attempt to jump - they both grabbed him at the same time as they were at equal distances from the subject, and put him through the window where we had gathered and watched.

The family, doctors, rabbi and hospital people assembled in the room, expressed their pleasure by giving us harrahs and applause. His mother kissed and hugged him as the doctors took charge of him. The doctors also praised us for our performance and thanked us. It was "Mission Accomplished" - "All's well that ends well!" He was crying out of control; I looked at him and said nothing as he departed.

It was now 4 A.M. - fourteen hours on the fourteenth floor. We were tired, physically and mentally, as we prepared to leave. I walked alongside of the Chief of Department as we made our exit, and told him I wanted him to excuse me from the 9/6 tour tomorrow, that I was here since after my tour was up at 6 P.M. Can you imagine his reply! He said, "I can't do that!" I was shocked by his answer, tired and upset with the prior performance of "Mr. Repulsive," and now I was being rebuffed by the Chief of Department for a tour off!

That did it! I angrily let him know that all he had to do was have his aide do the necessary - get a replacement for me on the 9/6 tour - it was that simple! I told him I wouldn't get home to bed till 5 A.M., and he wanted me to be back at 9 A.M.? This was contrary to reason or common sense and ridiculous! I then told him to rescind my acting deputy status and send me back to my battalion, as I surely resented being treated this way.

He then had a change of mind. His aide was next to him while all this was going on. He told his aide to make the needed notifications to excuse me, which was done. He kept me in the division as acting deputy - nothing more said!

It was back to business as usual again; I was still acting deputy in our division for vacations and vacancies.

Our division commander and I were very close personal friends. He was an excellent firefighter and extremely well liked by everyone. I remember when he came to us, all the chiefs in the division on duty were called to his quarters for a "getting to know" him session. When I went into his office, he threw his arms around me and hugged me, we were so delighted to be working together again! The other chiefs looked on - what a greeting! We had worked downtown Brooklyn together for many years as young officers, when he was a lieutenant, and I the acting battalion chief. We shared many memories and had many bad fires together. He too, was a top notch student, and his rise in ranks was rapid; he also was on the chief of departments' list. We had a beautiful relationship. He later had to retire due to an injury - he died young.

The next in seniority became the new division commander. We too, went back to the Downtown Brooklyn days, when he was a young lieutenant, and I was aide to Chief Lyons. We also had worked as battalion chiefs in the same battalion, and our relationship was the best. My aide, who was with me for years, also knew him from previous years, so all looked good at the time. We saw many changes in his attitude; he was now quick-tempered, fast talking, extremely authoritative and argumentative. As division commander he made many enemies with his subordinates, and it didn't take too long for us to get into it! I heard him chew out officers over the phone (in the division). It was repulsive to listen to him sound-off for the most trivial of instances. My aide and I found it most difficult to try to understand his vitriolic, bitterly scathing acid tongue. I couldn't believe this was the same person I knew! No one could approach him to have a reasonable discussion with him. I was no exception!

110

He phoned me one day when I was back in the battalion, and shouted and screamed at me for the most trivial thing - I was absolutely flabbergasted! I asked him what was wrong, and he kept saying I wasn't running his division! When I caught my breath, I wanted to know why he was chewing me out. I had put a small memo onto one of my reports indicating to the division aide the number of copies attached which were necessary. That report called for a different instance, and had been a source of confusion to many officers; some were two, three or four copies. When I got tuned in as to why he was so furious with me for such a thing, I told him I thought I was doing the aide a favor - why didn't he think likewise! What's the big deal! Again, another "from push to shove" took place over the phone, and he called me insubordinate. For the second time in my career, I heard the words, "I'll hook you up!"

I had a personal friend of many years standing, who was now an assistant chief in headquarters. We grew up together in the job, and had a great relationship as we were both buffs, and still liked to talk buffing with each other. He also had charge of assignments, and I called him, asking him to relieve me of the acting deputy job, and send me back to my own battalion. He was puzzled, but knew something was wrong, and didn't press me for any reason. I didn't give him any and he, being wise and understanding, didn't pursue it due to our friendship. In fact, he joked about my request, saying that there wasn't anyone else available to replace me - that's why I was there! We both laughed at that - he returned me to my battalion, and sent my battalion partner to replace me.

I had not visualized that, as I didn't want to give any headaches to my partner who was a dear friend and co-worker. He came back one day and told me the division commander asked him if I was crazy, giving up the detail. My partner said, "No - Eddie isn't crazy - he's smart! Wait and see how long I'm going to stay here!" He was right - he too got out of there.

My partner and I agreed that there was a pronounced transformation in the man's character and attitude - that a metamorphosis had taken place with many marked changes in form and mode of his lifestyle.

One doesn't need a degree in psychology or the study of mental behavior to know that this guy had a serious disorder, and was not functioning normally. His ability to deal with reality was impaired, if not altogether lost; he was totally aggressive and anti-social to everyone.

I reminded him of our many years of good relations, but he wouldn't stop telling me he would "hook me up." I told him to go ahead - make a trial case out of it - and hung up the phone. Minutes later he called me back screaming at me for hanging up on him. I told him we were disconnected! I did not want to go on with this any longer - I wanted it ended - it was ridiculous! His voice was rapid fire and he was not making any sense. I was upset, but tried to bring him around, and when I got the chance I asked him, "If you were ordered to forward an evaluation report on all the chiefs in your division, how would you rate me?" This apparently caused him some embarrassment - we had been close friends for over twenty-five years. I thought he must have been ashamed of himself, as he reluctantly said he'd get back to me, and hung up! That was the end of that. We barely ever spoke to each other after that, and kept a distance between us for a long time. He died in retirement and the ultimate inhumane, lack of pity remark was when his death was announced on the department orders. It was, "Where is his wake being held - in a telephone booth?"

The very next day I was visited by the deputy chief on duty. When quarters are visited by a superior chief, the procedure is that the housewatchman will sound a buzzer to the officer's and chief's office and announce his presence. The officer, chief and all men then respond to the apparatus floor.

I was sitting at my desk and the deputy chief gave a soft knock on my door and said, "Hi Ed." We warmly greeted each other as we were close friends. I said, "There wasn't any announcement of your presence - I didn't know you were in quarters." He told me he instructed the housewatchman not to notify us that he was here - this was a personal visit by him, to me. This deputy chief stood out as a first class gentleman. He had a great reputation, and was known as one of the best students in the job. He was articulate, always immaculate in appearance and presented the real image of a leader, which he certainly was.

He told me he was in the office and had heard me being chewed out. He said he couldn't believe what was being said to me over the phone and called it disgraceful. He had never heard anything like it and felt sorry for me, as I certainly didn't deserve the blasting I was getting. He told me he had seen my memo, copied it and put it in his rules book and complimented me for it.

We had a nice chat about our yesteryear memories and I thanked him for his consoling words. He said he just had to see me personally to tell me how wrongly I was treated. There were men like him of equal stature, but none better.

CHAPTER TWELVE

"YOUR FIREFIGHTING DAYS ARE OVER!"

I had several serious local fires, each resulting in my being injured. One was in a rooming house filled with smoke and difficult to locate the fire; I finally located it in the back of a half of a cellar in a crawl space. I was creeping along the space when out of the blue I got hit on the left side of my head. Fortunately I had a man with me, as I was knocked out and stunned. One of the truckmen had hit a boarded up cellar window open with an axe, to ventilate the cellar. I got the full impact - right on the head. I was taken to a hospital and placed on medical leave. I went back to full duty, and it wasn't long thereafter that we had a serious fire in a dwelling over a store.

It was 4 A.M. and a very serious potential life hazard existed. It was a good job done by everyone, as we got the occupants all out safely and extinguished a large volume of fire in the store, and superficial extension upstairs. During the course of examining the cellar, I fell into a deep pit which was not discernable to me as it was filled with water from our hoses used into the store above. My back hit the side of the pit when I fell. I later learned that a furnace had been removed, leaving a large open area where the furnace had been.

Off to the hospital again - x-rays and treatment and on medical leave. I thank God all x-rays were negative, but I had one painful lower backache for some time; in due time I was back on full duty.

Then it happened again - a simple fire on a roof - nothing to it. I went up the ladder and stepped off onto the roof of an old wooden building. The old rotted roof boards gave way and I went down the opening made hitting my back on the metal butt at the end of the ladder and the boards. My men on the roof saw it happen and heard the crack of the roof boards; they rushed to me, warning me not to move, as they thought it was my back that had cracked - actually it was the sound of the wood cracking. They removed me easily and got me down to the street. I was in pain and thought my hip and/or back was badly hurt. I was taken to the hospital emergency room and x-rayed, examined and released on medical leave. My back and hip area was badly bruised and turned black, blue and purple and was swollen. I was indeed lucky to be attended by the chief of orthopedics at the hospital. I stayed there until he was certain that all of the x-rays taken were negative. He was an extremely kind and considerate doctor, and his findings were that I'd be plenty sore for quite a while. Many hours later he allowed me to go home with instructions and to come back to see him for further evaluation.

When able to do so, I reported to the medical office and advised them accordingly. I told them about the orthopedic doctor, and I was told to stay with him and his orders for future care. After many trips back to the orthopedic doctor at the hospital, he advised therapy. The medical office went along with that and I went to the doctor's office for therapy treatments which lasted for a long time. I was placed on light duty by the medical office, and reported to the chief of personnel for an assignment. I was sent to our division to perform administrative duty there.

About three months went by and I received notification to report to the medical office for an evaluation of my injury. They sent me to an orthopedic specialist for his analysis and examination. It was a long, thorough examination. The next day the medical office had his report of the results. Then I received notification to report to the medical office to determine my fitness to continue to perform full duty.

I reported as directed and appeared before the medical board consisting of three doctors. They had all the reports from the hospital and the specialist they had sent me to. They were very kind and considerate to me with their questioning. The chief doctor said to me, "I have something to say to you." I had no idea what he was going to say and I said, "Fine, go ahead." He said, "Chief, your firefighting days are over!" I filled up and said, "Doctor, I am aware of that, but I'd much rather be in good shape and go back to work." They all wished me the best and I left the medical office with mixed emotions as I fully realized they probably would give me a disability retirement.

The department orders of their findings came very soon. I was granted disability retirement. The pension law provided that I could remain on the job doing "desk work" if I so desired. I made out "my papers" for retirement. After 33 years doing fire duty, I could not see myself sitting at a desk - it would be too drastic a change!

I had a peculiar, inexplicable feeling that I was retiring from the job I loved and was dedicated to. I thought the best thing to do was to make a clean, quick departure and avoid any sentimental goodbyes.

As I said before, retirement is a young man's dream, and an old man's nightmare. I began to wonder about many of the negatives, but I also weighed out the positives. The positives outweighed the negatives: no more night work, no more 4 A.M. runs, no more winter cold nights turning out, no more heat exhaustion during the summer, no more up all night at greater alarm fires and going home dead tired to bed. The list of "no mores" was very attractive - the time off could be spent at the beach surf casting, and at the race track now and then which I liked to do. My wife and I could take a trip to Florida during the winter, sleep late in the morning, etc., etc.

I remember when one of my chief partners retired. He came back one day for a visit and had a smile from ear to ear! He said to me "There's nothing like it - when you retire you'll enjoy the same feeling!"

I reported to headquarters to turn in my department property - book of rules, etc. It was a weird feeling sitting with my friend who was chief in charge of personnel, talking over old times. I am not ashamed to say we both were teary-eyed, as he said he was sorry to see me go and wished me the best. All of the paper work was completed and I left immediately. I didn't want any more goodbyes from anyone else.

I went to quarters to clean out my locker - it was another heavy emotional day. All the "no mores" weren't even thought of as one by one my guys came to the office for "so longs" and their good wishes. We had worked together for many years - this was the most difficult part of all - leaving the guys! The complete realization of knowing I'd miss them most of all, hit me hard. It was true - you won't miss the job as much as you'll miss the guys!

They helped me clean out. I gave most of my books

to a dear friend - lieutenant whom I had great admiration for and he for me. I gave my fire turnout coat to another lieutenant who also was a dear friend.

Finally - "Mission Accomplished!" I gathered my belongings and the guys helped me with them to my car. They asked me to be no stranger and drop in for lunch with them anytime. I said we would probably be away for awhile during the summer, but I promised I'd visit them. Again, more handshakes and good wishes from all, and I was on my way to the "no mores." I was "taking up" - "10-9" - off the air - off the job, after thirty-three years of service to the best job in the world!

My ex-partner told me there would be a testimonial dinner-dance for me on September 24th. He, a lieutenant and a fireman were on the committee. They let me know the date early, so I wouldn't be traveling any place. The Fire Chiefs' Association was behind it and mailed out the notices.

A Brooklyn paper had a notice about the coming affair. It read, "Ed Schneider, who retired last month as chief of the 42nd Battalion N.Y.C.F.D. will be given a testimonial dinner-dance at the Hollywood Terrace on September 24th by his former buddies in the department. It couldn't happen to a nicer guy (and we hope we didn't spill the beans)."

I had gone to many retirement parties over the years - some stag - some couples - they were fun. My wife and I also attended the social affairs of the many department associations, always having a good time. It was a strange feeling to be going to my own!

The evening came and my wife, family and myself were excited as we arrived at the Hollywood Terrace. The thought struck me this was going to be held in a

Battalion Chief Edwin F. Schneider (right) accepts a plaque from Battalion Chief Burns given in honor of his retirement from a 34 year career with the FDNY.

lovely new banquet hall - I also knew it was a large place - this made me wonder all the more! How come such a big place? I soon found out why!

We were met at the door by the committee who greeted us and kept chatting for a few minutes prior to bringing us in. The music started playing "For He's A Jolly Good Fellow," and we were escorted in to the playing and the crowd singing it. I froze in my tracks and literally couldn't walk my way to the dias. This large crowd was applauding as we marched in with our escorts and I really think I went into shock! I could not believe this was for me - I honestly thought I was attending some department social affair, as the crowd was cheering me! I was so affected and moved that I filled up and couldn't see - I only heard the crowd - I stood still - completely dazed - until my ex-partner took me by the arm to the dias where I stood practically numb, until the crowd stopped and we were seated.

It was a night to always remember. Speeches were made by the dignitaries on the dias extolling me as a chief and as a person. Of course I was embarrassed hearing them say such nice things about me. When I was called upon to say something, I thanked everyone for coming. I told a joke to try and break the ice for myself. I said when a wake was being held for a man, each friend, extending their condolences to the widow, would say to her, "He was a nice guy." She kept hearing it over and over and finally left her seat and walked away and said, "I wanted to know if they were talking about my Pat, or someone else!" I told them I felt as if maybe they were talking about someone else!

I thanked the Committee for doing such a splendid job. I reminisced about past experiences and events by telling a story or two.

The M.C. then presented me with gifts, and a plaque with shield. The gaiety, merriment, and dancing went on into the late hours - it was great seeing and greeting all who attended, as I table-hopped. We went home after a most cheerful and exhilarating night - thrilled to have had such an eventful evening with my friends.

Our local newspaper ran this story:

500 AT DINNER FOR EX-CHIEF OF FIRE DEPARTMENT - 500 persons turned out last Thursday night at the Hollywood Terrace to honor Edwin F. Schneider on his retirement as Fire Department Chief - Battalion Commander - of the 42nd Battalion.

EPILOGUE

MY FRIENDS
THE BUFFS

Of all of the memories of my long career with the New York City Fire Department, none are more cherished than those of the dedicated fire buffs.

Back in my buffing days at Engine 240 in Brooklyn, the men were practical jokers, forever playing tricks on each other, and me, too. One day the men did something, that after it was over, I gave it the name "The Blood Test." Had their doings not turned out the way it did for me, my buffing days would have been finished there, and anyplace else; I'm sure I would have been an outcast in their eyes, marked "lousy!"

It happened on a summer day in the afternoon. The firehouse entrance doors were open, the housewatchman was at the watch desk - I was on the sidewalk in front of quarters. There was an envelope laying on the sidewalk, right in front of the firehouse, practically at my feet. I picked it up and saw that it was full of something. A closer look revealed it was a bank envelope, sealed, with a fireman's name and the amount of his pay - it was payday. The envelope was so small that it bulged. I brought it right away to the housewatchman, who had full view of my finding it. I told him of my find, and said, "Chick lost his pay, I just found this on the sidewalk," and I gave it to the housewatchman. He went to the kitchen and gave the envelope to Chick (Fireman Gerrity), and I stayed at the watch desk. I saw the envelope being given to Chick, while the men looked on. Chick called to me from the kitchen, to come to him; he had the envelope - all the men were looking on. Chick thanked me profusely, and said it was his pay - he had lost it. He wanted to give me some money, but I declined any reward - my reward, I told the men and Chick was just to be allowed to "hang around," be their buff, and go to the stores for them.

All the men stood around the kitchen table as Chick opened the envelope. Of course, they were all in on it. Then everyone broke out in laughter - cut up newspaper fell out of the opened envelope! Some joke! When I too realized what actually took place, and they said they were watching to see who would "find the money," I didn't know what to say. Instantly, I knew that they had my trust, I had no doubt I had earned their respect for my honesty!

Many years later when I was a captain, I used to see Chick - he was aide to Boro Chief Raymond George. He respected me, as well as my rank; he was still a fireman. I looked up to and respected Chick. He was a fine man - peaceful and never hostile - a gentleman, quiet, a good fireman, and friend. There were all kinds of men in the job - introverts and extroverts - students and non-students - loudmouths (known as "Firehouse Lawyers") and the silent ones. I had an early introduction to mankind and it qualities, as I observed the different types. I am thankful I had the opportunity most of all to have known Chick Gerrity, whom I cherished as a friend.

One evening at Engine 240, an on-duty policeman stopped in for a cup of coffee, which was ordinary for the cop on the beat to do. The police and firemen always shared a common bond. The fireman on watch was a "firehouse jokester," and I was with him at the desk when the policeman came in and went to the kitchen. The housewatchman later on told me to "innocently" go to the kitchen and tell the cop that there was another officer who just walked in. I had to tell the cop this, but also let him know that the officer had a gold badge and stripes on his coat. I didn't like the idea of fooling around with a cop, but as their buff, I guessed I had to do as I was told. So, into the kitchen I went, telling the officer about the non-existing sergeant out front. It sure worked - better than expected - the cop jumped up, almost spilling coffee all over himself, muttering, "The sergeant's got me off post!" He dashed for the stairs which led to the roof within seconds, and stayed hidden on the roof of the firehouse. When I realized what could happen to me when he came down from the roof later, I didn't hang around to find out, I beat it out fast!

Many years later as an acting chief, and finishing up at a fire, I recognized the officer as I walked to my chief's car; we exchanged greetings and I told him we were leaving the scene, as our work was finished. This also gave me the chance to talk to him on a one-to-one basis. I asked him if he'd mind me telling him a story that happened years ago. I made him promise me by all that was holy, that he wouldn't get angry with me. Of course he didn't have any idea what I was going to say, so he responded, "Chief, whatever it is you are going to tell me, it will be strictly between us, and I won't get angry." "O.K.," I said, and then related the incident about the "Sergeant" that caused him to run and hide on the firehouse roof. When I told him that I was the kid who told him the "Gold Shield" was out front, he was speechless! He looked at me - the chief - the ex-kid who fooled him. I was sorry for the trick played on him, but the fireman on watch put me up to it. He regained his composure and couldn't stop looking at me - in disbelief! We shook hands, as he assured me he had no hard feelings, and he understood the firemen were always playing jokes on someone, just as they do at the police station. Amen!

As a small boy living in Park Slope, Brooklyn, I often saw a blind man walking, while tapping his cane. Time and again, as he would wait at the curb wanting to cross the street, I would go to him and cross him. I've always remembered him; he had a derby hat, mustache, dark glasses, and a cane. In time I got to know his name, and I'd say to him, "Mr. Schou, I'll cross you." When I was a lieutenant at Ladder Company 122 (Park Slope) there was a man there who was a life-long buff at the company. He was an outstanding gentleman and an executive with Pilgrim Laundry. He was always well dressed and well mannered. He lived in the neighborhood and would show up on his lunch break, during the day as well as at night. In time we got to know each other, and we became life-long friends. He told me he was an auxiliary fireman at Ladder 122 during World War I, and was buffing at the company since he was a young man. At that time I only knew his name was Larry. When I found out his last name was Schou, the name clicked, as I remembered the blind man's name was Schou. I brought up my childhood story of crossing the blind man who had a derby, cane, dark glasses, and a mustache. Larry told me that man was his father!

Our relationship grew over the years into a wonderful friendship. I regarded him as a close personal friend, and just about the greatest gentleman and buff I ever met. There were times when Larry would show up during the day for a brief visit, and then come back at night. I allowed him to ride with us to fires, as I had great admiration for him. Over the years I'd hear from him - by phone, letter, post card wherever he was, or a personal visit. Each promotion I received he'd be there congratulating me. He often visited me at quarters when I was captain and chief. He'd get a big thrill riding to fires with me in the chief's car and recalling our early days.

We'd go to fire department social gatherings together with our wives; as the years passed our friendship grew and grew. Through him I met some fine men who were also buffs. They'd invite me to their buff group meetings at their homes. They had ten members in their group, and each of us would put a nickel in a dish and select a number of the first stroke of the next box to come in over the F.D. radio. These friendships lasted all throughout the years I was on the job, and afterwards. Many of them would visit me at quarters when I was on duty, and ride with me; like I said, "Once a buff, always a buff!"

When I was a lieutenant at Engine 269 in Park Slope, the company had an elderly, wealthy buff. He was an honorary deputy chief, and we had a good relationship. Jokes were still a great pasttime then, as they had been for years. He lived in the neighborhood and would come around often for his evening visit.

When he was told that I was on duty, he'd come to my office for a chat. I found out that when he was told that Neal Donovan, the captain, was on duty, he wouldn't stay. He had many strange ways, one being he didn't take to the captain. I found that difficult to understand because the captain and I had been young firemen together at Engine 282 and Ladder 148. He was extremely patient, very intelligent, and well liked by the men. He was so smart we nicknamed him Einstein (proven correctly) - he went on to be a deputy chief. I always attributed my success in the job to him; he was a wonderful teacher always willing to share his knowledge with all.

My relationship with this buff was a strange one. I was very young - he was way up there in years. As we sat in my office, he would always reminisce about his early days. He loved to explain his inventions to me, which included a standpipe, water tower, and a substructure pier fire device. Of course, I was a very good listener, and he liked that.

One evening, we decided to play a "confidence game" on him, which we had done many times before to a newcomer. We had worked on it to perfection, and I was the "innocent" main performer to the gullible victim. Coincidentally, we had pulled this off on Captain Donovan - he never stopped laughing about how we fooled him. That game on him evened up the score for me on another joke played on me when we were firemen. He got me good because I fell for it only because of my trust in him, that he would never be part of fooling anyone, especially me! He had convinced me into believing that what they were going to do (a three man lift!) was a fact. When they got me as the victim, all I could say when it was over was, "I knew it - I knew it!" (Neal and I always greeted each other as, "I knew it!") and had many a laugh over it.

The con game on the buff took place in my office as we were talking. It was simple and easy to execute. All that was needed was a soda bottle top, and a sheet of paper.

The bottle top had cork in the bottom. A piece, the size of a dime, was cut out, to snugly fit the dime. The dime was placed on the plain sheet of paper with the rigged bottle top placed over and holding the dime. This was similar to the "pea shell game," with the victim turning up the shell where the pea was supposed to be. The set-up was for me to remove the dime from the paper, as the buff watched me take the dime, and leave only the bottle top supposedly covering the dime. Bob Shanley, one of the men, would turn his back to this, as I lifted the cap, and take the dime.

The buff's eyes were glued to the sheet of paper. He saw me take the dime from under the bottle cap - he was ready for the "rip off!" Now the fun really began. Bob would bet he could remove the dime from under the cap, and not disturb the sheet of paper. The buff knew that was impossible to do, as he knew I had the dime in my pocket. How could anyone remove the dime, when it wasn't there? He bet it couldn't be done, and out came his money - we had him hooked! All of us in on it played it cool; we didn't have but ten dollars, we told him. He wanted to bet his roll, but settled for a ten dollar bet. I said I'd take two dollars of the bet, while the others covered the remaining eight dollars. Fireman Shanley then tapped the cap, which caused the dime to fall out of the cork onto the paper. He then lifted the cap, removing the dime, without disturbing the paper.

The buff thought he had beat us out of ten dollars - after all, he trusted me - and never dreamed I'd be part of the scheme. We howled laughing as we picked up our winnings and watched the look of disbelief on this wealthy buff's face! He was speechless! When it sunk into him that he had been "clipped," he was furious and plenty angry at all of us, especially me! He was yelling what a dirty trick had been played on him as he got up from his favorite club chair and started to storm out of the office screaming at all of us. I had all I could do to calm him down, as we gave him back his ten dollars and told him it was all in fun! Finally, he cooled down and accepted the fun by laughing with us. He gave one of the men the ten and had him go to the store and buy us sandwiches, soda, and ice cream! P.T. Barnum surely said it all, "There's a sucker born every minute!"

When I was a captain at Engine 226, and later a chief, the wealthy buff would often visit me at my quarters; we'd recall the fun we had, and both enjoyed a hearty laugh. Fireman Shanley became my driver and aide when I was a chief, and remained as such all throughout my years in the rank until I retired. He was a wonderful man, a good friend, and an exceptionally good aide and fireman. We had great times working together and shared many memories and laughs about the past.

The old wealthy buff and I had many disagreements. It was truly a case of his living in the past and of me applying the great saying of Lieutenant Gregory, also of Engine 269, "New men, new methods!" Amen!

The old buff had a big Cadillac car and a private chauffeur whose name was Joe Traub. Joe was also a buff with us on his time off. He was a real dyed-in-the-wool fire buff, a man in his early fifties, quiet, fine and easy to get along with. Joe was liked by all of us and was always making himself useful around the firehouse. I allowed him to ride with us; he would help by stretching hose, assisting the chauffeur in hooking up and getting water on the fire, and also be on the line with us. He'd tend to the furnace, go for our stores, and was an asset to us in many ways. He did all of the things I had done as a young buff; he never overstepped himself or took advantage of his "hanging around." His job as chauffeur to the old wealthy buff had no influence on any of us - we liked Joe for being just a nice guy and a good buff.

One evening on our return to quarters from a fire, we were near an intersection at Grand Army Plaza with a green light for us. As we were approaching Flatbush Avenue, going slowly, a trolley car on Flatbush Avenue, which was standing still on a red light, went through the red light. Our driver, Ed Hicks was one of the best in the job. We always were most observing of conditions in the streets, and both of us at the same time saw this huge trolley car coming right at us. Eddie swerved to the left to avoid a sure collision - he almost made it - but the trolley struck us at the right rear end near the back step. Just another foot more and it wouldn't have happened.

Joe, the buff, was on the rear step and was thrown off. He had on boots, helmet, and rubber coat, and looked just like any of the other firemen. He got up and ran for all he was worth into the park across the street, getting away from the scene. I was busy checking the men, and in the confusion of questioning the motorman and doing what I had to do, the men told me Joe had run into the park. There is always some confusion when there is an accident, this was no exception. The motorman was crying his head off - he told me he was so sorry he hit us, for he was late, and ran the red light to make up lost time! He couldn't control his crying! With all of this going on, Joe was now in the park. I had many things to do, getting all the needed information, and I was upset about Joe. This was a tough spot for me to be in. I didn't know if he was injured or where he was, but at least I knew he had run into the park.

We went back to quarters after I had obtained what was needed, and about an hour later as I was sweating it out about Joe, he walked into quarters carrying the helmet and rubber coat, and wearing his boots! The men downstairs called up to me in my office, saying "Joe is here, Lieutenant!" I slid the pole immediately and went right to Joe, who was at the watch desk. I was so glad to see him, and all I could say looking at him was, "Joe, are you allright? - Are you hurt?" He assured me that he was O.K. - he had a bruise on the leg! He told me he hid in the park and said to me, "Lieutenant, I didn't want to get you into any trouble for letting me ride!" I sure was relieved to know he was O.K.! That's a first class definition of a real good buff - he was looking out for me, not himself! Joe was "all man," and "ten yards wide" - I could never forget him.

These were the chances some of us officers took when we knew we had a good buff. It was no different than when Captain Casey had the guts to let me ride with him when I was a buff. There were officers who wouldn't allow it. Of course, I never faulted them for it, as it was a risky thing to do; a bad accident and injuries could happen, with no way out for the officer who'd get into plenty of trouble.

A friend of mine, a lieutenant, and I would often go for an afternoon walk together on our day off. We were both on the promotion list for captain, and we were probably due to be promoted in the very near future. When I got home, my wife was anxiously waiting for me, excited at what she had to tell me. She said Deputy Commissioner Butenschoen had telephoned several times, wanting to speak to me. He gave her his phone number and told her to have me call him when I returned. That was the message - no more, no less - and I was really concerned why he'd call me at home.

He used to be our division commander when I was Chief Lyon's aide as a fireman. He was, without any doubt, one of the best liked of the decent, kind, men in the job. He was now First Deputy Fire Commissioner and I had absolutely no idea what he wanted me for. When I returned his call, I tried to think of some reason, but I turned up a blank. I identified myself on the phone to his secretary, and was immediately connected to him. In his always gracious, kind, courteous manner he said he wanted me to know that I was to be promoted to captain tomorrow morning, and asked me if I had a company in mind that I'd like to go to! I was flushed with excitement, and thanked him no end for his kindness. I was flabbergasted and surprised by his call. I told him I knew there was a captain vacancy at Engine 226, as my friend who was captain there, had just retired. His answer to me was, "It's yours, Captain!" The next day I was promoted and assigned to Engine 226; thus began another chapter in my career as I moved along in the job.

I was familiar with Engine 226, as I had been temporarily assigned there as a lieutenant for six months, while attending officer's school at the Fire College. I knew the men there, and the company was known as a hard working unit. Chief Butenschoen was very pleased with my asking him for the company. I thanked him personally after promotion ceremonies.

At Engine 226, there were four buffs. The men and the buffs were glad I was their "skipper," as we knew each other from my previously being a lieutenant there. In retrospect - recalling the past years - Engine 226 was a "hitch" of many pleasurable, enjoyable, fond memories, which could never be forgotten; thank you Chief Butenschoen - "Destiny at work again!"

Buff No. 1 was Dr. Harry Vinecomb. He had his office near our quarters and worked out of Brooklyn Hospital nearby. He was affectionately called "Doc" by all of us. The years were catching up to Doc, and he was approaching semi-retirement. He had been the company buff forever, starting there as a young doctor. He never failed to make his daily visit to us at the firehouse - he truly loved seeing us - and we enjoyed his company. Doc was a lovely gentleman, kind, well mannered, and always enjoyed a laugh.

Buff No. 2 was another fine elderly gentleman, named Harry Deegan who worked for the gas company. He was called "The Dep," short for deputy. Both he and the Doc were buffs at Engine 226 for fifty years. These two fine men would never go upstairs to the kitchen, as they were happy and content to sit in their chairs in the cellar, forever talking about the big fires they had been to. I always asked them to the kitchen for coffee, but they always politely refused. They'd talk about the horse-drawn days, the steamers, the old time skippers of Engine 226, and shared their memories. Many times I would join them in the cellar and attentively listen to their tales of yesteryear, as they drew comparisons between "the old days" and present times. Both were up in years and facing retirement, but never lost their enthusiasm for buffing.

Buff No. 3 was a fine young man named Harry Monahan. He had buffed at Engine 226 for years, and was the credit manager for A. & S. Department Store, which was around the corner from our quarters. He'd always hear us responding and would show up at fires, helping in any way he could. During many of the 6 to 9 tours at night, Harry would buff and ride with us, and then go to his job at A. S. in the morning from our

Engine Co. 226 as it exists today.

firehouse. I allowed him a bed at quarters - he wasn't married then. He was (and still is) a great buff, and a good, decent man, plus my friend. Harry later moved on to a higher position in a big store in Philadelphia; he moved to Jersey, got married, has a lovely family, and our visits became fewer and fewer. I haven't seen him in years. He always was, and always will be a true buff - he joined the volunteers in Jersey.

Buff No. 4 was my dear friend, Allan Plumer, a fifteen-year old black school boy. I had met Allan before when I was a lieutenant, and he was so glad to know I was now the captain of the company. Allan was a fine young boy who went to school during the day, and buffed with us in the evenings. His mother was a widow, and whatever change he'd make from us going to the stores, he'd give it to his mother when he got home. He was very religious, intelligent, and the most honest, trustworthy lad anyone would ever know.

These were my four buffs; each was a beautiful person. Many times I had to use all the persuasion and wisdom that I could muster, to pacify Allan - and the men - to resolve their differences peacefully. You see, the men here too were also "jokesters," at times at Allan's expense.

Harry Monahan and Allan both went overseas during the war. Allan became a firefighter in the army. Harry became an infantry officer. They had many stories to tell us when they got back, and continued buffing. When our good friends "Doc" and "The Dep" passed away years later, they left this vale of tears with a part of all who knew them. They left their marks as buffs at Engine 226, as wonderful, polite gentlemen - true and beloved by all of us. Rest in peace!

I had a two-piece engine company at Engine 226, a 1000 G.P.M. Ahrens Fox pumper and a Walters hose wagon. At outdoor drills we'd practice laying two lines from the hose wagon, one into the deck pipe, and the other a hand line into the building. Repeated performances for the purpose of acquiring skill at this paid off many times when it was called for at fires. We were a top notch unit, had pride in our company, and enjoyed a good reputation.

Doc and the Dep never wanted to ride with us, but Harry and Allan always did. Allan would ride the hose wagon sitting next to the chauffeur, and be the bell ringer en route. In those days, nearly everyone in nearby units knew each other. Time and again I'd hear someone say, "When did 226 get a black fireman?" It didn't take long before Allan was known as a buff with us, and enjoyed being said hello to by the men from other units. He was proud and pleased with the recognition, and I as the skipper, felt the same way - I had good buffs, and a good outfit!

After the war, Allan was discharged from the army, and came right back to us, continuing his buffing. I told him a police examination would be held soon, and he should take it to gain the experience for the soon-to-be-held fireman test, as the police and fire exams were similiar. He told me that while in the army, he had to wear glasses, and didn't think he'd pass the eye test, and better not go for the police exam. I told him that if he didn't file and take the exam, I wouldn't allow him to be our buff anymore! He needed encouragement, and I had to give it to him. He was stunned that I, his friend, would say that, as buffing and riding with us was his whole life. It didn't take him too long to say he'd take the exam. He filed, took the written, medical and physical, passed, made the list, and was appointed a patrolman in 1948. The day he graduated from the police academy, he received his shoulder patch - a horse's head - as he was assigned to traffic. His girlfriend, Sylvia, later his wife, and Allan, came to 226. She sewed his patch to his uniform coat in the kitchen of 226. It was a great day for everyone, as all of us in the company helped him prepare for the test. He directed traffic at Atlantic and Pennsylvania Avenues - a very busy intersection - and was there until he retired twenty years later.

Sylvia and Allan bought a house in Queens, and raised four children. She knew how devoted he was to buffing, and never minded him doing it. He buffed with us when he could. Ladder 107 was near his post, and he soon got to know the men there; it wasn't long before he was buffing and riding with them, on his day off! He also buffed at communications, and became an auxiliary dispatcher. Another definition of a "true buff."

When the next fireman's test was held, Allan decided to pass it up. He was still buffing and riding at Ladder 107, was happily married to Sylvia and raising a family. All and all he was doing quite well. He often visited me at my chief's quarters, and I'd take him with me on runs. We'd have lunch together in the kitchen, and in no time at all enjoyed the men's talk, and they in turn were happy to have the chief's buff tell his stories about me!

I like to tell one particular story about him. When we arrived at a fire one day, Allan quickly got out of my car and ran like a rabbit towards the fire premises. He was very agile, young and in good physical shape. Two uniformed policemen at the scene saw him running and they grabbed him. I had to tell the cops he was my friend, and buff, and a brother policeman! Allan showed them his shield and identified himself. The two cops looked at him in disbelief, a cop riding with a chief! Everyone had a good laugh, the cops, me, my aide - all except Allan. He saw the humor in it later on and it remains one of our "stories to tell," to this day. We hear from each other now and then; we are both retired, and treasure our many years of friendship.

One day tour at Engine 226 I was very sick with fever, and was in bed in my office. The men knew it, and when Doc Vinecomb showed up for his visit, the men told him. He came up to my office - I believe that was his "first ever" time he was upstairs! He examined me and said I had 104° temperature. He gave me medication from his doctor's bag, phoned my battalion chief and the medical officer from my office. He reported me sick right then and there, gave me a prescription and sent me home in a cab. That evening I had a 105° temperature, as my wife waited for our family doctor to arrive. I was later told that I was delirious. My doctor loaded me up with penicillin, and stayed with me for a long time. My wife had told him about what happened at the firehouse and Doc Vinecomb taking care of me. I was fortunate I had Doc, my buff, attending me as I was very sick, and was in no shape for fires or smoke. Many times Doc took care of other emergencies at quarters. Once a fireman had a severe laceration; Doc was there at the time and fixed him up. He did many good things for all of us, really too numerous to relate. He gave to us, and we gave to him - respect, kindness, consideration and most of all devotion to each other.

There was a fine young man named David Klein who buffed at my chief's quarters. He was extremely polite, refined, and willingly did all he was asked to do. He was always doing something useful around quarters, and was well liked by all of us. He worked for a large department store in the Bronx, and would buff with us on evenings and Sundays; he was a devout admirer of us, and oh, how he wanted to be on the job.

The time was approaching for an entrance examination, and one evening I told him so. I was excited telling him, and thought for sure he would be delighted to know it. Tears were actually in his eyes, he was heartbroken as he told me he knew the test was coming up, but wasn't going to take it. He was married and had a young baby; he told his wife about the coming exam, and she was positively adamant against him wanting to be a fireman! She told him that if he went against her wishes, she would take the baby and leave him! She didn't mind one bit that he buffed with us - that was OK - but no way was he going to be a fireman! I tried in vain to console him remembering how I, at his young age, wanted the job just as he did. His wife had her way, and he never took the test. He stayed buffing with us, and became successful in his work. Again, fate and destiny at work.

We had another buff there who was a confirmed bachelor. He was in his fifties, and was a cab driver; we called him "Harry the Hack." He worked his cab days - and would be with us all night. He had two pastimes - his love of buffing, and deep sea fishing. Everyone got fish when he went fishing. He was so different than young David - the "older" and the "younger." Harry would sit in the kitchen all night, telling us "fish stories," while David would always be doing something useful around the house for us. They were both liked and accepted by all of us - they were as different as night and day, but truly good buffs in every sense of the word.

The term "buff" originated many years ago, when buffs were first called "buffalos." During the cold winters, they wore coats made from the hides and fur of the buffalo. As the years went by, the word was shortened to "buff," which they are still known as today. They were also known as "jakes" and "vamps."

Long before there were organized groups of buffs, there was a firehouse buff, who helped the firemen at a fire, and brought them coffee. They helped in picking up hose after a fire, and would have coffee ready when the men returned to quarters. During the winter they would tend to the firehouse furnace, making sure there would be warm quarters and hot water for the firemen upon their return. The buff would close the entrance doors when they responded, keep out unauthorized persons, and watch over the vacant firehouse. He'd pick up the scattered shoes laying around the floor that the men had kicked off to put their boots on. It was not uncommon to return to quarters and find shoes and articles missing; the buff prevented such losses.

Fire buffs come from all walks of life; some are men who could not qualify for the job; others share the devotion of liking the atmosphere of the job. Many are doctors, lawyers, judges, clergymen, brokers, and professional men.

Many men have devoted their entire lives to buffing, from boyhood to manhood. Today, there are some women buffs following the engines, taking action photos at fires. We had a registered nurse called "Smokey" who was in charge of a hospital emergency room; she'd show up at a working fire with her first aid bag, and many times gave treatment to injured firemen. There was a violent explosion on the docks one day which caused many deaths and injuries to workers. Smokey was credited with saving many from bleeding to death.

Suburban and rural areas throughout the country have volunteer fire departments. Volunteers were once called "vamps": - "Volunteer Association For Mutual Protection." Many of these volunteers were buffs in the town's fire company, before coming of age to join the company. They "chased the engines" for the men, and eagerly awaited the day when they came of age to join the company and be a "volie."

The community volunteers are in a class by themselves. They give of their time freely fighting fires without pay. They leave the comfort of their homes when the siren sounds, and take great pride in the job.

I have the highest respect for the nation's volunteer firefighters. Buffs and volunteers - I salute you!

ABOUT THE AUTHOR

At age 82, Chief Edwin F. Schneider and his wife, Rita, still live in Brooklyn.

Ed attands many of the anniversary parties and reunions of the outfits he worked in and commanded, and he enjoys reminiscing with his pals of yesteryear.

Other Books By FBH Publishing

Fire Service History Series

- **Chemical Fire Engines** *by W. Fred Conway*
  The only book ever written about the amazing engines that for 50 years (1872 to 1922) put out 80% of all fires in the United States.

- **Fire Boats** *by Paul Ditzel*
  The definitive book on the history of marine firefighting by the "Dean of Fire Authors."

- **A Century of Service** *by Paul Ditzel*
  The official history of the City of Los Angeles Fire Department, the second largest fire department in the world.

- **Fire Alarm!** *by Paul Ditzel*
  The fascinating story behind the red box on the corner. A history of fire alarm telegraphy with emphasis on Gamewell.

Civil War Series

- **Corydon — The Forgotten Battle Of The Civil War**
  by W. Fred Conway
  Only two "Official" Civil War battles were fought on northern soil — Gettysburg, and ... Corydon. Two thousand Rebels invaded the North on captured steamboats.

- **The Most Incredible Prison Escape Of The Civil War**
  by W. Fred Conway
  "The Thunderbolt of the Confederacy," General John Hunt Morgan, tunneled under the granite wall of the Ohio Penitentiary in a dramatic and thrilling escape.

- **The Ruthless Exploits of Admiral John Winslow – Naval Hero of the Civil War** *by Paul Ditzel*

- **Quantrill – The Civil War's Wildest Killer** *by Paul Ditzel*

American Heritage Series

- **The Incredible Adventures of Daniel Boone's Kid Brother – SQUIRE** *by W. Fred Conway*

- **Young Abe Lincoln – His Teenage Years in Indiana** *by W. Fred Conway*

FBH Publishing, P.O. Box 709, New Albany, IN 47151
Phone 1-800-457-2400